Living In God's Glory

Hearing & Responding to God's Voice

Supernatural Experiences of
Dudley Perio

As told to Paul & Lynn Crawford

†

New Sound Media

Kingston, WA 98346

Living In God's Glory: Hearing & Responding to God's Voice. The Supernatural Experiences of Dudley Perio

Copyright © 2011 by Dudley Perio

Published by
New Sound Media
PO Box 7300
Kingston, WA 98346
godshealingpower@gmail.com
www.OneInTheSpirit.tv

Please note that our publishing style capitalizes certain pronouns in Scripture that refer to the Father, Son, and Holy Spirit, and may differ from some publishers' styles. All Scripture quotations are italicized, although not always put in quote marks unless someone is speaking. When noted, Scripture versions are identified by acronym as follows:

ISBN 978-1-4507-3544-5

For Worldwide Distribution, printed in the U.S.A.

2 3 4 5 6 7 8 9 10 11/15 14 13 12 11 10

O Sovereign Lord! You made the heavens and earth by your strong hand and powerful arm. Nothing is too hard for you. ... You have all wisdom and do great and mighty miracles. You see the conduct of all people, and you give them what they deserve. You performed miraculous signs and wonders in the land of Egypt—things still remembered to this day! And you have continued to do great miracles in Israel and all around the world. You have made your name famous to this day.

Then this message came to Jeremiah from the Lord: I am the Lord, the God of all the peoples' of the world. Is anything too hard for me?

They will be my people, and I will be their God. And I will give them one heart and one purpose: to worship me forever, for their own good and for the good of all their descendants. And I will make an everlasting covenant with them: I will never stop doing good for them. I will put a desire in their hearts to worship me, and they will never leave me.

—Jeremiah 32:17-20, 26-27, 38-40 NLT

Endorsements for Dudley

Natalie Perio (Dudley's wife): For years it's been the cry of my heart and the prayer of my lips that Dudley would love the Lord with all his heart, mind, soul, and strength. I have faith that God's love for us and our love of God is the unfailing answer for all of our challenges and problems. Sometimes it takes time and with Dudley, time and more time. But I have witnessed God's love heal, mend, release, blossom and bear much fruit in Dudley—and through him to others, including to myself and our kids.

He totally amazes me with: his faith in God and God's power; his quick forgiveness towards himself (very important) and others (just as important); his desire to encourage; and his heart to help others. The glorious love of God is working in him.

And then the gold dust! At times, we had seen gold dust on our hands, clothes, and chairs during worship at church. Now, it was showing up on his face, neck, chest, arms, and hands. He washes it off and it comes back again. Boy, is that something! It has caused my mind to spin and my heart to cry, "Lord, what is this about?"

It is one thing if it is happening to someone else but this is my husband. The days of "gold dust" have been surrounded with testimony after testimony, most happening to people simply as Dudley goes about his daily life. And I heard the Lord say to me: "God wants His glory on the streets.

Dudley is carrying gold dust (God's glory) outside the church walls and among the people. People have been and will continue to be touched. What an adventure in God!

Daniel Perio (age 32): When I first heard of gold dust showing up on my dad I was skeptical. However, having witnessed this appearing in person has opened my eyes to how "real" miracles can be. My dad leads by example when it comes to living the Christian life. God's putting this "gold dust" on him has given him more opportunities to share Jesus with others.

Sarah Perio (age 30): What can I say about my dad? Well, he is funny. There is always laughter when he is around. He is inventive, kind, and courageous. He is one of the most generous people I have ever known. When we were children, I knew my parents were struggling financially, but my dad would always say, "I have money I haven't even spent yet." We would all laugh, someone would cheer, and someone would inevitably say, "I hope so." He has a way of lightening moods and always gives us confidence and reassurance that everything is going to be okay.

His trust in the Lord taught me to trust—as I saw God come through every time. I have learned a lot about my Heavenly Father through my dad's life and his love for God. I think it is a beautiful thing that God is working mightily through my parent's lives, but I know He has even more ahead and I look forward to what He has in store for them next.

Nathan Perio (age 27): I have such an amazing father. He has continually supported me in my life's quest and cheered me on in whatever I've done. He believes the best in me. He is a man of such simplistic faith in God and his life story is example after example of it. He has modeled for me loving and giving from a pure heart and not expecting to receive something in return.

That has only continued when the "gold dust" started to appear on him. When people ask, he always points them to God and then gives away what he's been given. To me the gold dust is a sign that simply points to an unexplainable God that is really good. Why it is happening doesn't really matter to me as much as what is coming from this situation. And all I can see is that God is being glorified in my dad and in the lives he is touching.

Kenny Perio (age 26): At the time of this writing, Kenny is a Sergeant in the US Marines and deployed to Afghanistan. He is currently out on a mission. Therefore, we could not get his response in time for printing. We are very proud of him and all those who serve our country. Their unselfish service to protect others truly reflects our God. (written by Dudley)

Natalie Ann Perio (24): It has really caught me off guard—something like this happening to someone so close to me. It is easy to say that I believe in all of this crazy supernatural stuff. But when I heard it started happening to my dad, it became such a reality that it actually challenged me at first. I caught myself trying to reason what it could be. But God has once again shown me that He is outside of any box I could make for Him. Now, I am truly amazed at the realness of our God and His goodness—not only towards my dad but through him. I am taken back when I think about where my dad has come from—to where he is now. The only answer is: the Love and Power of God. I am so excited for him and what is to come for our family and beyond.

Clara Perio (22): Over the years, I have known my dad to be in many unbelievable situations where he made a decision to go past fear, step into faith, and create a place for God to move. This is one of the major things that I look up to in my dad.

For me, the "gold dust" continuing to be on my dad isn't a surprise or shock—it's the things God is doing through this in people's lives that are unbelievable. It is amazing how God is encouraging people just because He loves them and no other reason. That's what makes my heart burn. So since I am my father's daughter, I am looking for my inheritance of these encounters of God's love and looking for Him to show up in crazy ways. I love my dad!

Contents

Dedication

I dedicate this book to my loving wife, Natalie, and my amazing children, Daniel, Sarah, Nathan, Kenny, Natalie Ann, and Clara. I thank God for their endless prayers for me, and for believing in full-faith that God answers prayers.

Their covenant with God has truly protected me all over the world. Their walk with God has carried me through the deserts and storms of life. Just like God, they never gave up as I was learning to be a father, husband, and a servant of the Lord God Almighty.

They taught me the true meaning of "counting it all joy" (James 1:2). Their love of God is a true reflection of His nature. When I felt I was not worthy, they never ceased in pouring out their love.

I thank God for giving them a faith beyond measure. In our days of plenty and our days of drought, their love never wavered.

In the many weeks and months I spent away traveling the world in the oil fields, they never forgot to pray for me.

In the storms and floods of life, they surrounded me with their encouragement, allowing me to walk on their ceilings and catch my breath.

—Dudley Perio

11

Foreword

Paul Crawford

Over the last thirty years, Lynn and I have seen, experienced, and lived in "God's glory." These manifestations (God revealing himself to believers, John 14:21 NKJV) have included: gold dust, glory clouds, feathers, angels, oil, gold teeth, gems, and worship that connected us to God's throne.

We have seen and ministered healing of most sicknesses, diseases, afflictions, and creative miracles, as well as regeneration of cells of the body that do not renew themselves naturally.

This ministry has taken us over 2.4 million miles, more than one hundred international trips to teach seminars and produce recorded media at more than 900 Christian conferences.

Sometimes, we think we have seen almost every way God manifests Himself on earth today. Then we came across something or someone new: Dudley Perio in Austin, Texas.

When I met Dudley and heard his story (fifteen days after his gold dust manifestations started in September 2010), I saw another aspect of God's glory.

I was producing an eight-part video series called, "Creating the Atmosphere for Healing, Miracles, Grace, the Supernatural" and four more.

The DVDs were produced in a private home over two days. About thirty people attended the recordings. The group changed almost hourly as some would come and others needed to leave.

Dudley walked in just before we started recording the session "Creating an Atmosphere for the Supernatural." We began that taping with an interview of Dudley.

We all witnessed the gold dust (or flakes) appearing on his body as he worshiped and entered into God's presence. He told us that daily showers removed it, however the gold dust would return a short time later every day.

The intensity varied from hour to hour and day to day. There have now been over a hundred days of this heavenly demonstration. Since Dudley is an "outdoor guy" the public is exposed to his "gold dust" manifestation daily.

The reactions are varied, but most interesting from unbelievers, like "hey, dude, you really know how to party" or "what is that all about."

His answer is: "When I experience God's presence with me, this happens." This has led to hundreds of ministry opportunities mostly initiated by unbelievers.

Many Christians have problems with God's manifestations—like gold dust, oil, or feathers. Some Christians seem skeptical. Others don't want to know what it's all about or believe it could be happening today.

When we have heard Heidi Baker or David Hogan telling about someone being raised from the dead, you can see many Christians in the audience with questioning looks, as though to ask, "How dead were they?"

God's manifestations of His glory in group services, or through individual one-on-one meetings, are a dramatic faith-building experience for those who believe. Sometimes we are more prone to believe, only accompanied with a *little* doubt.

We include a lot of Scripture in our book to scripturally support what we write. Over the last few years we are seeing manifestations of God's glory that we don't find specifics about in Scripture. I want to give you a gold tooth example from my experience.

I produced media at a worship conference in Moravian Falls, NC some years ago. Most of the speakers I had known personally for many years. The assistant to the conference director, Bob a retired pastor, had a molar that needed filling. The dentist appointment was for the next week. Bob had roomed with me at another conference. He and his wife conduct children crusades around the country.

During the worship service, a few people sensed something in their mouth. On inspection they had a tooth that was now gold. As they streamed to the stage for verification, I saw Bob. Bob had a gold tooth, where the infected one had been. I saw his gold tooth, as well as many other people who received gold teeth that night.

Many of the supernatural manifestations we've seen over the last few years—and are now following—have occurred through the ministry of people in their twenties.

Jeremy became a Christian at age eighteen. When I first recorded him, he was twenty years old. My first reaction was about his knowledge and revelation from the Word after such a short time in the Lord and the Word. And then I couldn't help but notice the notable healings and miracles in his meetings.

There are about a dozen of these young men that I currently record their ministry. They have one thing in common: They turned everything over to the Lord. And they asked for everything of God for themselves.

I wish I had done that. Instead, like many of you, I laid down a piece at a time. It has taken me over fifty years—laying down problems I am dealing with to come to the spiritual maturity these young men received almost instantly.

Dudley got this concept when he said, "God I will do your work if you will do mine."

Some people have not understood what Dudley was declaring. He was saying: "I will serve and minister as you direct me if you will supernaturally help me do my engineering job." He turned his life completely over to God.

> *I will pour out my Spirit upon all people.*
> *Your sons and daughters will prophesy.*
> *Your old men will dream dreams,*
> *and your young men will see visions.*
> *In those days I will pour out my Spirit*
> *even on servants—men and women alike.*
> *And I will cause wonders in the heavens*
> *and on the earth—blood and fire and*
> *columns of smoke.*
> —Joel 2:28-30 NLT

Lynn and I wrote a book and now teach seminars called, *God's Healing Power Through You.* It is based on Mark chapters 16-18 where Jesus says: They (believers) shall lay hands on the sick and they shall recover. I think the New Literal Translation says it best: The Believers who *BELIEVE.* The church is full of people who believe partly, which is unbelief.

There are fakes, counterfeits, and enemy manifestations, so we need to test the spirit.

What is being manifested through Dudley has led to many words of knowledge, healings, and miracles.

After staying in Dudley's and Natalie's home, getting to know their pastor and close friends, and testing the spirit, I know that Dudley's manifestations are from God.

Additional re-enforcements for my belief are the expression of God's love, and the humility, in which Dudley walks. He gives all the glory to God.

In almost every respect, Dudley is an ordinary man. He has world recognition, as an oil field engineer because of his inventions and technology, which he credits God giving to him. Isn't it interesting that Jesus also chose simple fishermen for his disciples—ordinary men who would obey and follow him.

Lynn and I find it easier for people to believe supernatural manifestations today than the people did who lived in Jesus' time. For many around Jesus, it was hard to accept this ordinary young man, as Jesus, the Son of God. Some believed, but some did not.

This will be the same for some reading Dudley's story. Some will believe, and some will not. Lynn and I do believe.

Our prayer is that this book will give you a broader view of God (let Him out of the box you have had Him in), your faith will be enlarged, and the supernatural power of God will flow through you.

> *For God, who said, "Let there be light in the darkness," has made this light shine in our hearts so we could know the glory of God that is seen in the face of Jesus Christ. We now have this light shining in our hearts, but we ourselves are like fragile clay jars containing this great treasure. This makes it clear that our great power is from God, not from ourselves.*
> —2 Corinthians 4:6-7 NLT

Preface from Dudley

This book is for all my back row buddies, who were dragged to church by their wives, or came just to please them. We bonded for years. And to all who are struggling through life's sometimes hard journey. To all those who need to see God move, but feel you're not qualified because you aren't pastors, you're real people, living in the real world. Life doesn't seem fair. And some of the people you work with could teach the devil a few things. To the people who say, "I'm not in the clique. I'm not seeing a move of God, and life just doesn't seem fair"—this book is for you. I hope as you read each part of the book, you can feel my heart, and you'll know, I am a real guy.

Sometimes I think life is like a golf game. You can choose to take your putter out and go from the tee to the green, tee to the green, and play the entire game your whole life. God is real, and if you ask Him, He'll give you a driver. You can then sail over your hills and bunkers and get there fast. He'll lift you up and cause you to live in His power in your life and touch the lives of all those around you.

Then you will realize "How great and mighty is the Lord God Almighty, and how worthy He is to be praised."

I pray for each person who reads this book, that all that God has given to me, you will receive. I pray the power of God in your life releases the full restoration of David. A restoration so complete He even takes away the painful memories which have marked the hard places you've walked through.

I pray these miracles impart into your daily walk and you pass them all to everyone around you. I pray the light of God's glory shines so strong that everyone around will see Jesus in you. And then miracles, signs, and wonders will follow you everywhere you go.

May God bless you, may God hold you. As you walk through the testimonies written here, may God touch your heart with what I have seen as a real guy who walks with a real God. May I be hidden in Him and to God be all the glory.

—Dudley Perio
Austin, Texas

1

God Provides A Job
March 1994

*And this same God who takes care of me
will supply all your needs from his
glorious riches, which have been given
to us in Christ Jesus.*
                              —Philippians 4:19 NLT

Thirty-three years ago, I started in the oil field industry as a welder and in the equipment fabrication business. In the oil field, my assignment was to design and build equipment, all different kinds of equipment. The work was outdoors in all different kinds of weather. I went to engineering school and became an engineer for a company designing equipment.

I have six great children so it's always been a priority to make enough money to survive. It's always been my drive to be the provider for the house. The oil field jobs are long hours and through the years there has been a lot of traveling.

As I was striving to get ahead, I didn't want someone else raising our children. I wanted to provide so my wife would be able to raise our children with great morals, great understanding, and with great compassion for people. I wanted us to be their guidance.

Because of the time required away from home, I missed out on a lot in my children's lives. But I was doing what I had to do. I'd been taught the man is to be the provider for his family. It was up to me.

I wanted to give my children more than I had when I was a child. I believe people need to work hard.

I worked with intensity so I would be seen as a top oil field worker. When I was informed I'd received a raise, the first question in my mind was: *What do I need to do to get the next raise?*

I've had design abilities from the start— changing equipment, modifications, designing new equipment, and being able to do it quickly.

God had been guiding me with direction and inspiration, but I'm sorry to say I didn't always give Him the credit I should. I took the credit.

I loved my wife and I believed in God and Jesus. I believed it was Jesus and I. I didn't need anyone else. I didn't need the church. I believed God was there, but to get something accomplished, I'd have to do it.

I would go to church but in essence my wife was dragging me there. I was smart enough to know that "if mama ain't happy, nobody's happy." So I decided I would sacrifice my time and go to church to keep peace in the family.

My primary view was that the pastors were not living in the real world. I was going to work and he was going into a church that was providing him a nice livelihood.

I believed there were anointed people, but not in the oil field. In the oil field, men don't mention God. Well, they do, but there are a lot of words coming before or after His name. I saw that some of the oil field workers were not living right but were succeeding. People in the oil field and people in the church lived in two different worlds.

On the way to church, I'd have a family meeting and tell them: "Five minutes after church is over, I want you all out here in the car." We'd go to church and put on nice smiles.

I was careful not to get there early. It is funny to think about it now because I know God was involved. The ushers would save the closest parking spot to the front door, so I could be the last one in and the first one out. They also saved me a chair in the last row in the back of the church. In this last row of chairs, I was assured of being the last one in and the first one out.

Now I was in church with nothing to do. I would sit flipping through the Bible pages, looking at the maps, and trying not to fall asleep. They'd only have one service, I hoped. I wanted to get out early because the football game was on.

It seemed like the pastor and everybody in the church was perfect. Perfect hair, perfect suit—everything perfect!

Then I'd go to my oil field work and everything was not perfect.

But as long as I attended church, Mama was happy.

As a child, I had very little exposure to the church. My parents were divorced. When we were little we were Catholic, but not really raised Catholic. We simply attended the Catholic Church. My siblings and I made the march to church every Sunday.

My mom worked two jobs, so she primarily went to church on Easter and Christmas. One time we all went on Easter Sunday morning, but when we walked in, the priest would not allow my mom to enter—because she was divorced.

It hurt my mom and it hurt me. I thought: *That's not God, anyway.* We wanted to cry out to God when we needed Him, but we didn't understand how we could.

After that incident, we quit going to church and I didn't want anything to do with church.

I wanted to marry someone who loved God. I wanted someone who could teach me about God. I've never had an interest in reading the Bible for myself. I thought it was only words. I am certainly not a Bible scholar. And I still don't know the Bible as well as I'd like.

I wanted my children to know God because I knew He could come through for them in difficult times. I only wanted God at certain times.

But as I went through life, I could see God's hand move here and there. I thought I had to provide for my family, but I didn't have to trust God. I knew He was there, but I couldn't trust Him.

I knew I couldn't trust myself to keep all the commandments and not do wrong. I heard the sermons and believed God had a big measuring stick. I knew I would make a mistake. I would blow it. I couldn't live the "good lifestyle."

I thought a lot of sermons did not apply to me. I believed I had the "fire insurance." I loved

God and believed I would go to heaven. I felt that was good enough.

I met an old school friend, but I knew I was not good enough for Natalie. She knew God. Every time she talked, it seemed like she wasn't talking like an ordinary person. At times she would slip up, but most of the time she was only speaking well. I married my friend.

I would see "spiritual" things happening but tell her, "Honey, this is not real, wake up."

She would say "try this" and that was why I went to church. She was full of joy and I didn't want to rob her of that joy. I also didn't want our kids to miss out.

I tried to do a few of the things she said I should try. I tried to pray in the car, but then I would get slammed with a problem or be offended. It wasn't the same in the oil fields as in the church.

Natalie was an inspiration to me. I would call her from work when I got hurt and ask her to pray for me. As a welder, I often got burned. I would say "let's pray together" because I knew God would hear *her* prayer. She became my source of connection to God. I didn't think God was listening to me.

She has always been a rock for me. I was trying to understand God's love. I could see it in her but I couldn't see God move enough to trust him.

A turning point for me was when I lost my job and had a period of unemployment in 1994.

We had a little bit of money in the bank. I could see in her eyes we needed to trust God. So finally I told the Lord, "I will give you a shot."

All of our efforts were focused on getting me a job. After the first month, there was no job.

I have never been on unemployment compensation and "Praise God," I never have to this day. I was too proud to apply for unemployment compensation.

Then came month two—nothing! At the end of month three, I was ready to give up on trusting God with Natalie. We were keeping the situation away from the children so they would not be worried.

I went into the garage, started pacing, and said, "God, I trusted you. This is not working. I trusted you and I still don't have a job."

"Don't say that," my wife, Natalie, said. She did not waver, she didn't give up.

Natalie was worried that my unbelief statement about trust may have cancelled out the spiritual progress we had made over the past three months when we were trusting and believing God would provide the job I so desperately needed.

But I was in conflict. I knew God was real. I knew He kept His promises. But it just wasn't happening.

The next day I received a call from our competition offering me a job. I took it, even though it meant a weekly commute from Austin to Houston.

God came through for me, for us. It was not a great job but it was a job designing equipment. This company had sold an oil drilling platform, for ocean drilling, to go overseas.

Soon I was promoted to Project Director to build the equipment. God led me in the design of it. Because of the completion time requirements, the equipment and I were shipped to Norway to finish the construction.

Therefore humble yourselves under the mighty hand of God, that He may exalt you in due time, casting all your care upon Him, for He cares for you.
                                —1 Peter 5:6-7 NKJV

2

Trading Jobs with God
September 1996

That night God appeared to Solomon and said, "What do you want? Ask, and I will give it to you!"
— 2 Chronicles 1:7 NLT

The new job made me so thankful. I had a new longing to be closer to God, so I would try to pray in tongues the whole way from Austin to Houston, or I'd say "Praise the Lord!" whenever a car passed me.

My job is to design equipment for the oil industry, all kinds of things. God gives me the designs and inventions. I "see" them in my mind. I am amazed. These are things I've never seen before. Quite a few patents have been filed on the new inventions He's given me. Early on, I didn't give Him the glory. I was taking the credit. But that was all about to change.

This company sold an oil rig to Norway to operate in the North Sea. They used some of my designs. We had a year to put it all together. The deadline came and we still weren't done. They decided we should complete it in Norway, in the dead of winter. I've never liked cold weather but just like that, I was on my way.

My employer promised I'd only have to be gone three weeks max. No more than six weeks at the most—guaranteed. What that became was a fiasco. We were breaking new ground with the hydraulics, but it was slow going. It seemed every time we took a step forward, something else put us back two.

I called Natalie and told her about our set-backs in getting this rig up and running. It was the first of its kind.

She suggested I anoint it with oil and pray over it. So I did. I was ready to try anything.

The Norwegians didn't think prayer would help. They told me, "God doesn't like us." They thought God was putting all these obstacles in our path. They didn't know then how much God wanted to bless them.

Time just seemed to pass day-by-day, problem after problem. As soon as something worked, I would take the credit.

Then, WHAM! We'd be hit with another problem.

✝

On September 16, 1996, I was driving to my apartment in Norway frustrated as usual with our progress that day. It was 9:30 p.m. when I stopped at a stop sign standing in six feet of snow.

"STOP!"

It hit me like a ton of bricks. It knew it was God saying stop.

"OK, God, enough is enough. I'll trade jobs with You. God, if you do my job, I'll do yours. My way's not working."

God took me up on my offer. The next day when I got to the work site we were still having problems and we couldn't find the source. We checked the manufacturer's drawings on the valves and everything was right. We went over every inch again and again. It should have been working, but it wasn't.

That night I gave the situation over to God, went back to my room, and color-coded the whole hydraulic schematic, which is a sheet about 3 ft. by 3 ft. with hundreds of lines about a quarter inch apart. It shows the entire hydraulic flow circuits of the rig. I had a multi-colored pen, so I colored each individual line with a different color or color combination.

When I talked to Natalie the next morning about the struggles we were having, she said, "The Lord told me it's a blue line."

She didn't even know I'd color-coded the design and amazingly it had only one blue line on the sheet.

I went to the blue line. There was one valve on that line, so I pulled up the manufacturer drawing. It all checked out.

At 10:30 a.m. we started taking that valve apart. When we did, we found it hadn't been manufactured according to the drawing. There was a check valve in there that was blocking the whole system. Instantly, we were up and running.

Earlier, when the Norwegians had asked me how long it was going to take to get the rig up, I'd told them twenty-four hours, not realizing that was the Lord's leading. Two of us and a crane operator had this rig going in twenty-three hours. That was the beginning of the successes to come. God was taking care of my job. He's so good.

Norway is a socialist country so there are not many opportunities to learn about God, not much Bible teaching. There is an occasional street evangelist on a corner spouting hellfire and brimstone which just turns people off.

So I invited a couple of guys to my apartment to share God's love with them. It grew to thirteen people seeking after God every Thursday night. Before I left, I encouraged them to check things out in the Bible, and find two or three verses that agreed with what they were hearing. God was moving among us.

One day we had a pin drop off the rig floor, which is about thirty-five feet above the ground. At the base of the rig there was a big cellar that would catch all the spills of hydraulic oil. We were pumping 7,600 gallons a minute. That's a tremendous amount of oil. If there was a problem, we would have a big pool and fill up the cellar.

We would hire a company to come out to suck all the oil out of this pit. On this day, one of their men was bent over working. Suddenly, a pin about twenty-seven inches long and ten inches in diameter, weighing three hundred pounds, rolled off the rig floor and fell straight down toward the back of the man who was bent over. We all turned and saw it just as it came over the ledge. There's no doubt it was going to kill him.

Immediately, I stuck out my hand and yelled: "Jesus!"

The pin turned as it was falling and completely missed him. We all saw it. The pin's trajectory changed. It missed the man.

The Norwegians, the Danish, and the Swedish observers all saw it and were astonished.

"What happened?" they asked.

"That's God," I told them. "He loves you. He loves us. He's protecting us. This is His rig."

By this time, I was giving *all glory* to God for His wondrous workings. I was a worker for Him in this environment of twelve to thirteen hour days, seven days a week. My attitude was "Thank you, God, I can work for you today right here, even in this bitter cold."

And it was cold. The gauges were guaranteed to 40 degrees below, and five times we had to replace the gauges. We could only be exposed to that extreme cold for about fifteen minutes. Then our lungs would start freezing up. We'd have to go in a container where we'd light toilet paper and diesel to warm up. We could get the temperature up to about 30-34 degrees to stop our lungs from freezing up.

This rig became a success, the first of its kind, causing quite a stir in the industry. The major oil companies of the world were coming to get a look at this rig. Colleges in the United States sent people over. Major hydraulic companies from the USA and Germany flew to Norway to see how we got this thing to work.

"It won't work. It can't work," they said.

Then we'd show them it did work and they'd still say they didn't understand. It went beyond the "laws" they were familiar with. No one had ever seen anything like this. God was getting all the glory!

He reveals profound mysteries beyond man's understanding. He knows all hidden things, for he is light, and darkness is no obstacle to him.
                                    —Daniel 2:22 TLB

But there is a God in heaven who reveals secrets.
                                    —Daniel 2:28 TLB

3

The Rock Changed Directions
September 1997

*Jesus told them, "I tell you the truth, if
you had faith even as small as a mustard
seed, you could say to this mountain,
'Move from here to there,' and it would
move. Nothing would be impossible."*
—Matthew 17:20 NLT

The job in Houston was proving to be very
good. I needed it with six kids to
support. We put in long hours Monday
through Friday, starting at 5:30 a.m. and we
usually didn't finish up until 7:00 p.m. With
Austin a three-hour drive each way, it just
wasn't practical for me to go home every night.
I couldn't afford the time or the money.

I wanted to rent an apartment month to
month, but they all wanted me to sign a one
year lease. I couldn't do that since I'd heard the
Lord say, *"Don't sign a lease."*

39

Searching out the best lodging deals, costing around $40 a day, meant I was in a different room every night. Finding that room and moving my stuff every day was a hassle, but I was already learning it's better to be obedient, even if that means being inconvenienced.

✝

"How do you hear God?" people ask me.
"I spend time with Him. I've learned to recognize His voice," I answer.

Jesus said: *My sheep recognize my voice. I know them, and they follow me.*
—John 1:27 MSG

Instead of listening to the radio in my car, I praise Him. Sometimes I make it our game to see if I can say, "Praise the Lord" whenever a car passes me. I thank Him for everything. I pray in tongues. I sing in tongues. I even get a little loud sometimes. I'm free. Free to worship, I'm not holding anything back, but I make sure to keep my eyes open when I'm driving.

Celebrate God all day, every day. I mean, revel in him. Make it as clear as you can to all you meet that you're on their side, working with them, and not

40

against them. Help them see that the
Master is about to arrive. He could show
up any minute.
—Philippians 4:4-5 MSG

God began teaching me about intimacy. I'd just be quiet. Even my inner dialogue is dialed down so I can hear Him speak.

He's never condemning. His love and peace fills every word. One of His names is "The Prince of Peace" and His divine peace is incredible. It stills the voices in our head and the fears in our heart.

Don't worry about anything; instead,
pray about everything. Tell God what
you need, and thank him for all he has
done. Then you will experience God's
peace, which exceeds anything we can
understand. His peace will guard
your hearts and minds as you
live in Christ Jesus.
—Philippians 4:6-7 NLT

Since the night I switched jobs with God in Norway, there's been an urgency in me to share His love everywhere I go. I know I'm not God, but I desire to do as much of God's work around me as I possibly can.

What's around me? I'm in the oil field business, and let's just say you won't find a lot of church-goers and pastors in this line of work. There's long hours and hard work. Oil field workers are a tough breed. I know these men. I am one of them.

I didn't have the Bible memorized, chapter and verse. Sometimes I still have trouble with that. Usually the Lord just brings to my mind the Scripture I need for the particular situation. If I need the Scripture "address," Natalie can help me find it. She really knows God's Word!

What I did know was that God loved my co-workers as much as He loved me. And I knew how to talk their language. I could see there were guys here He wanted to reach. I was the perfect man for that job.

Could this be another way God is keeping His promise that each of us will hear the gospel in our own language?

There were some religious Jews staying in Jerusalem who were from every country in the world. When they heard this noise, a crowd came together. They were all surprised, because each one heard them speaking in his own language. They were completely amazed

at this. But we hear them telling in our
own languages about the great things God
has done!"
—Acts 2:5-7, 11-12 NCV

God is good. He leads us by the hand, step-by-step. He wants to be glorified in our real everyday life. I racked up a lot of miles in this season of our journey. It wasn't easy staying in motels. My nightly calls to Natalie helped. But still, being away from her and the kids was really tough.

I had this inner "knowing" that my time with this company was almost up. But I wasn't about to make a move until God told me. I couldn't let the loneliness or difficulties pressure me into stepping out on my own.

Tuesday morning was a bright morning. As I woke up, I realized it was one year to the day that I changed jobs with God. I had to meet with a customer at his facility on the outskirts of Houston.

I headed east on the Interstate. Traffic was moving along nicely so I wasn't concerned when I found myself surrounded by eighteen-wheelers, one behind me and one on each side of my Toyota 4-runner.

Then I saw three boys on the pedestrian over-pass up ahead. They had a big rock, eight to nine inches in diameter and, in a split second, they threw it right at me.

I realized there was no way I could swerve to avoid it. I was boxed in. I threw my hand up and yelled: *Jesus.*

Instead of gravity pulling that rock straight down on top of me, in mid-air its path altered. The rock veered off to my right. Instead of a direct hit on the driver's side, it hit the passenger's side and cracked the windshield.

The rock moved! Jesus caused that rock to move! If it had hit me, I'd probably be dead. But Jesus intervened and the rock moved!

I was so pumped. I wasn't worried about my car. I wasn't even mad at those kids. Just like He had moved that pin for us in Norway, Jesus moved the rock!

I was so excited, I couldn't even think straight. I went on to my appointment. When I met the customer, we went outside to my car.

"What happened to your car?" was the first thing he asked.

"The rock moved!" I said.

He wasn't as excited about it as I was, but I didn't care. I could barely even think about the parts they were interested in buying.

I'd just witnessed a miracle, and that overshadowed everything else.

I stayed the day at the customer's facility, and decided to get a room for the night since it was so late. What a great day, I was so excited about what God had done!

4

Motel Warfare Fight
September 16, 1997

Be strong in the Lord and in his mighty power. Put on all of God's armor so that you will be able to stand firm against all strategies of the devil. For we are not fighting against flesh-and-blood enemies, but against evil rulers and authorities of the unseen world, against mighty powers in this dark world, and against evil spirits in heavenly places.
—Ephesians 6:10-12 NLT

By 5:30 p.m. that same night, I was settled in Room 136 at the Motel 6 right by the airport. It was still light outside, so I kept the curtains open as I stretched out on the bed reading a book. At 9:15 p.m. I glanced at the clock. It was now dark outside. BAM! I was jolted by a huge bang on the door.

Did someone just kick my door?

The kick was so powerful I could actually see the outside lights shining through a gap between the steel door and the frame. I jumped for the door. But before I could even reach the knob, it burst open.

Suddenly, there is a gun—a long-barrel .38 revolver—pointed at my upper right thigh. A huge man, towering between six-five and six-seven is holding the gun in his left hand. A mountain of a guy, he appeared to be 285 pounds of solid muscle. He is foaming at the mouth, his head tilted back, and he is shrieking like a banshee.

I'd never seen anything like it. His eyes are messed up. They don't even look human.

"Give me my wallet!" he shouted.

This would be funny if it wasn't happening to me, asking for *his* wallet instead of *mine*. This is like a dumb criminal "reality" show on TV, but it's happening in real life—*my life!*

I raise my hands in total surrender and stand frozen in fear. *I'm probably going to lose my leg.* I try to calm him down and befriend him.

"Hey, buddy, you can have my wallet. I don't have your wallet, but you can have my wallet, my car, whatever you want. I won't tell any-body. I won't call the cops. We can keep this just between us," I said.

"Give me *my* wallet!" he repeats at the top of his lungs.

"I'm going to kill you!" he screams, as he holds the gun in his left hand.

He began moving the gun upwards on my body. As it passes my heart I'm thinking, *I'm going to die.*

My right hand grabs the gun, my thumb under the barrel, and my fingers hold the hammer down.

The gun flies to my forehead between my eyes. I can see the scratches in the grey lead of the bullets in that revolver just waiting to be fired.

He is squeezing and squeezing as he tries to get off a shot, but my grip is preventing it from firing.

[I need to explain here that our family, including Natalie and my girls, have done tae-kwon-do together for years. The whole family is "black belt" level. Our family plans were to leave in two days for a competition, so I'd been in training and I was in pretty good shape.]

Fighting this guy is like fighting a brick wall. I am hitting him with everything I have in my left hand. Because I have the barrel in my right hand, I only have my left hand to defend myself. I hit him so hard I feel the spine in his neck. He doesn't budge. I gouge his eye, rip his nose, rip his mouth. I cannot move him. I use a kick-move to get the door closer to me.

I begin smashing his head between the door and the door jamb. Nothing is working. He continues to try and squeeze off a round. I haven't moved him even one inch.

This is all happening in the partially open doorway. People are standing outside watching. The manager has been doing his rounds, but he is frozen there, too afraid to move.

On the other side of the parking lot, two elderly couples have just checked in. They are petrified, like statues. Later they said the fight lasted a full five minutes. It seemed much longer to me.

The attacker is still screeching.

"Jesus, Jesus, Jesus," I'm yelling. I'm desperate and getting tired. Very tired. *I can't do this much longer*, I'm thinking, but maybe it is more of a prayer. *If I let go of the gun, I'm dead.*

I know I have to get the gun off my forehead. In a last ditch effort to survive, I grab the door and manage to move my head behind it. Then I slowly slide my head away from the gun.

If it goes off, it'll blow the side of my head off, so I'll probably still be dead, I reason. Yet all the while, I'm still yelling: "JESUS! JESUS!"

Then as my cheek is flattened against the door, I look up towards the ceiling and it has disappeared.

I am on the ground floor, Room 136, of a three-story motel, and there is no ceiling. I am looking right into space, outer space, and it is so huge and so beautiful. It seems surreal, like I am looking into deep space from the bridge of the Star Trek Enterprise. It is so magnificent!

"Did the gun go off?" I ask myself. It hadn't. I could still feel the barrel in my hand.

Maybe it did go off and I'm dead and I just don't know it yet.

I could still feel the barrel in my hand. No, it has not gone off.

What is going on? I'm fighting for my life. I'm at the end of my strength. Why is there no ceiling? What is happening?

> *For He will order his angels to protect you wherever you go.*
> —Psalms 91:11 NLT

All of a sudden there is a mighty "swooping" sound as angels charge into the room.

Immediately, a shapeless black glob, about three-feet tall pops up from the floor and the battle is on.

Each time an angel swoops in, one of the black things pops up, and they begin exchanging blows.

The angels are gold in color, yet I can see all their muscle structure. I can look right through

51

them. Some have wings, some don't. They are all between twelve and fifteen feet tall. Their faces shine with power. They don't appear male or female. They have no weapons or shields. It is all hand-to-hand combat.

The angels are hitting and going at it as the black things strike back. The fighting is intense. A fight to end all fights.

An army of angels fills the room. It seems like God sent in angelic reinforcements to protect me and combat the enemy who's not giving up.

I am beyond astonished. The fight is still on when suddenly a brilliant light begins beaming from the back of the room. I turn my head to look over my shoulder. I hear a voice that is all authority.

"You will not take these children's father," the voice said.

I felt about two inches tall, like I could sky-dive off a skid mark on the street.

God sent an army of angels, not because of me or anything I was doing, but because of my children.

God was honoring the covenant for my children's sake. It is a hard place to be in.

It wasn't exactly what I was doing that was the issue. It was more about what I wasn't doing.

I'd surrendered most of my life, but not all. I was still limiting God's control of certain parts of my life. God wanted me to take the full journey. I was still putting God in a box, and only pulling Him out when it worked for me.

"Call upon my name," He said. (Keep in mind I was still physically fighting this guy, still yelling "Jesus" at the top of my lungs.)

"I am! I am!" I yelled back to God.

Then I felt like I was suddenly within a sphere. My hearing was so acute I was no longer limited to just one conversation. I could hear and comprehend Him from all 360 degrees.

All around me, God was speaking into me. He imparted knowledge to me of things to come, things that would happen, things I could and could not share. I was immersed in Him.

Then He said, "No, call upon my name. In the name of Jesus."

So I said, "Go, in the name of Jesus—GO!"

And just like that, without me touching him or hitting him, my attacker instantly folded up and went shooting out the doorway. I see him soar through the air even though I haven't moved him an inch. He didn't land on the side-walk or where the cars parked. He landed in the center of the parking lot.

Later, witnesses said it looked like when a cartoon character is blasted out of a cannon, except this was no cartoon. This was my attacker.

I slam the door and lock it as fast as I can. My room is still full of angels and Jesus is in there, but I want the door secured.

Then I hear: "Come unto Me."

This is just a regular single motel room. There are still many angels and black things fighting like crazy. It is crowded. I carefully make my way to the back of the room. As I get to the back, I hear the voice again speaking to me.

"Stand upon my Word, and I will stand in front of you."

Looking down I see what appears to be a "pillar of words." It looks like a transparent cube, 2 foot by 2 foot by 1 foot tall, filled with floating sentences. They move constantly, filling the entire cube. As I look at the pillar, I see the verse: *Nothing shall by any means harm you.*

Two weeks prior to this incident, I was in church but I was bored and not really listening. I picked up the Bible. After the maps, there were no more pictures to hold my interest. I started flipping through the pages. When I got to a certain page, the words appeared to be levitating above it.

This is cool. Some kind of misprint made this hologram effect, I thought.

"Nothing shall by any means harm you" (Luke 10:19) floated above the page.

Natalie was engrossed in the sermon, but I whispered to her, "Look, Honey, these words are floating above the page."

She glanced at my Bible and didn't see anything unusual, so she just shushed me, like only a wife can, and fixed her attention back on the sermon.

I've never been into memorizing verses except for, "In the beginning ... and the Amen." But this verse stuck with me. Our God is good. He was preparing me beforehand for this very moment. And that one verse was all I'd needed.

Now, in the back of the motel room, I stepped into the pillar of words. Instantly, my arms go up without my even telling them to. I really wasn't into raising my hands in church. I thought God didn't need me to put my hands up. But now, I'm standing there, my arms up and I don't think anything of it.

In the meantime outside, the attacker gets up off the pavement and comes back. He starts pounding on my door with his gun. He hits the metal door so hard, all the while screaming, "I'm going to kill you!"

In spite of everything, I am standing in the pedestal of God's Word, confident Jesus is in front of me.

"If you stand on My Word, I'll stand in front of you," He told me. I'm counting on it. God's divine light is beaming out of the window of my room like crazy.

Now, the attacker comes to the window. The light beams illuminate his face.

It is just single-pane glass, not bullet-proof. He takes his revolver and he starts hitting the glass with everything he has. He seems determined to get to me one way or another. He's trying to smash the glass and he should've succeeded. But God is reinforcing that glass and it is impenetrable. I knew even if he did shoot at it, the bullet would not go through it.

Nothing shall by any means harm you.

A police car rushed up and two officers jump out, drawing their weapons and shouting, "Drop your gun!"

The attacker raised his hands and tosses his gun down. The officers approach and grab him by the arms, one officer on each side. They holster their weapons. Then just as they are putting his hands behind his back to put the handcuffs on, he breaks loose. The fight is on again!

Another police car pulls up and another and another. They are all fighting him. It takes thirteen well-trained officers to restrain him.

I am still just standing there. God's light is beaming all around. The angels and the black glob things are still fighting.

Once the man is in police custody, the light cleared. The room appeared normal, just four walls, and a ceiling. I didn't see angels anymore —just me.

A police officer motions for me to come out. The first thing I see is this huge guy, double-handcuffs on his feet and hands, surrounded by thirteen officers.

The police separate me, the manager, and the two elderly couples to get our statements. I go with the sergeant, while two other officers go inside to inspect my motel room.

One of them comes back to the door and asks, "Where's the photographic equipment?"

"What?" I said.

"The equipment. The photo equipment. Where is it?"

"There's no photo equipment," I answer.

"Yes there is," he insisted. "We saw the bright light beaming out of here when we pulled up. We thought you must be filming something."

"Well. There's no back door. And I just came out. You can see there's no photo equipment in there."

"How many people are in the room?" the sergeant asked.

"Well," I said, "It was me, Jesus, and about one hundred angels."

"Whoa!" he said. "Hold on a second." Then he called his partner to join us.

"There's something I need to tell you," he said looking directly at me. "I don't know how we are going to write this up. I've been on the force eighteen years and nothing like this has ever happened to me before. Whatever ... I need to tell you something."

Then he turned to his partner and said, "If I say anything that isn't correct and the absolute truth, I want you to take your gun out and shoot me."

"Wait a minute," I jumped in. "Let's put the guns down and keep them down. Enough is enough."

"Because Houston has four million people the shift changes are very specific," the sergeant began. "Whenever any of us has a shift change, we immediately go straight back to the station. There's always another two officers waiting for the car. This is standard operating procedure. Once we get the call, we make the change and we head straight for the

58

station. There's no stopping unless it's a matter of life and death.

"We were on our way back to the station when we both heard a voice coming from the back of our car. It said with authority, 'turn around.' We looked at each other and then we looked in the back seat to see if somebody had snuck in. The seat was empty. We looked at each other again. Then without a word, we turned the car around. As we were driving, the Voice would say, 'Go left' or 'Go right.' When the Voice stopped, we were in front of your motel room. This isn't even our district, but that's how we got here."

Then one of the policemen checking my room came out. "Where can I get some of that cologne?" he asked.

"I don't have any cologne. I don't use it," I said. (But if you were to take the most expensive perfume, it would have reeked compared to the scent in my room. It was the heavenly fragrance of the Lord.)

Then one of the officers found a bullet on the floor. It had two impressions from the pressure of the firing pin. But it was intact and had never been fired.

Police later identified my attacker as a truck driver who was a competitive body-builder. He had taken steroids, crack, and alcohol. They theorized he'd had enough of life and wanted to commit mass murder starting on one side of the motel and working his way down.

"Fortunately, he started at your door," the officer told me. "You should have been dead. It took thirteen of us to get him down, and you fought him off with one arm."

My attacker needed medical treatment, but I didn't.

I tried to buy that motel room door, but they wouldn't sell it to me. I think they were worried I wanted it to sue them or something.

I checked out of the motel that night, as did all of the witnesses.

This was another life-changing pivotal moment for me. *This encounter changed everything.* Now I was on fire for God. No holding back. I was going after a relationship with God like my children have. And I would take it to everyone I could.

"The devil planned for you to die that night," my pastor told me, "but God planned for you to live."

5

Teaming Up In The Spirit
September 1997

*We do live in the world, but we do not
fight in the same way the world fights.
We fight with weapons that are different
from those the world uses. Our weapons
have power from God that can destroy the
enemy's strong places.*
                    —2 Corinthians 10:3-4 NCV

Natalie's Story: I didn't know it but I
was in intercessory prayer at the exact
time the spiritual battle Dudley was in
was going on in the motel room.

I was at a prayer meeting—intensely battling
in my spirit the whole time. My prayer language
was authoritative and commanding, not the
usual tranquil river expressing love and
adoration. During this prayer time, I believed I
was battling for the Body of Christ. I didn't
know it was for Dudley.

An intense seriousness and pressure came upon me. I sensed God needed me to focus and go into intercessory prayer right then. I yielded completely. I gave my all—body, soul, and spirit —to this call to battle in the spirit, mostly praying in tongues.

"Where's Dudley?" I asked the Lord, as I left the prayer meeting around 9:15 p.m. I was wondering if he was at the motel or might be staying with friends.

In my mind's eye, I saw beams of light shooting about, going swoosh swoosh. The Lord often gives me pictures, but this one was different. I didn't understand what it could mean—until later.

Even though Dudley travels a lot and I'm home taking care of our children, God has made us one in the spirit. Our unity is not diluted by the miles or time zones between us. The bond of the spirit we share makes us function as a team.

Even when Dudley was living in Norway and we were communicating via long distance, we almost seemed closer in many ways. Instead of the everyday stuff we can all get caught up in, we focused on the most important—God and us—and we trusted Him to help us with the rest.

At this point in our relationship, we certain-ly had our challenges, but God was working in our midst. We desired unity, so God was growing us in that direction.

Dudley's Story: This is not a one man band. It's about family and true unity in His Name. Not just by denomination or location, but joined together in "His name" and doing all for the glory of God. Like Scripture tells us: Loving God with all our heart and loving our neighbor as our self (Matthew 22:37). That's what it's all about.

We sometimes make compartments in our lives. God fits over there—but where I'm struggling over here is my part.

God wants to overflow into all of those compartments and be our everything. We get in between Him and our struggles. He wants to get in there with us to help us, not to condemn.

Over and over He's saying, "I love you. I need you. I need you. Help me."

I know that seems odd, God wanting our help. But we have a physical body. He can love through us when we're hugging someone, or heal through us when we lay hands on people.

We're always asking God for His help. We're forgetting to ask: "God, how can I help you?"

I'm in the oil fields. I always thought that if I was a pastor or a teacher or someone special then I could live a godly life. But I'm living in a dog-eat-dog environment. It's the real world with men fighting for position. If you go up to one of these guys saying, "God bless you," they're likely going to take you out. I'm an everyday ordinary guy, but God wants to show many people how His grace extends beyond church walls.

I'm authentic. I'm real.

God is blessing me in my regular everyday life and struggles. I don't know why God is using me in these miraculous ways. God is good. He wants to use all of us. He likes to take ordinary people and accomplish extraordinary things!

6

Money, Mystery, Miracle
December 1997

For your Father knows the things you have need of before you ask Him.
—Matthew 6:8 NKJV

When I was inside "God's sphere" in the motel room (where God's influence had complete control of me), He told me a lot of things that would happen and would not happen in the future. We were in huge debt at the time. One of the things He told me was, "You will be out of debt within ninety days."

That seemed impossible to me, but God said it, so we believed it.

It came time for me to leave the company I was with. That didn't seem like the logical thing to do since we had so much debt. But I just knew my time with them was up and I needed to trust God completely.

"Go register a company name for the state of Texas," I heard God say.

So I drove to Austin from Houston to do just that. When I arrived, parked, and stepped out of the car, there right by my foot was a crumpled $50 bill.

No one was around to give it to, so I picked it up and said, "Thank you, Lord," as I put it in my pocket.

Before the clerk could register the name the Lord had given me, she needed to check and make sure it was available. *Of course it was. God gave it to me.*

"We can mail this to you and it will take several days or we can express it for a fee and you can take it with you today," she said.

"What does that cost?" I asked her.

"Fifty dollars."

Of course it does! That wadded up fifty I found would just take care of that!

We were so in debt. I didn't have extra money for anything like that. But God did!

So now, I was in business! This was a notable miracle. It may not seem big to you, but God had said I would have my own business. And now I did.

The very next day, I sold a swivel, one of my God-given designs. A swivel is a device that goes on an oil rig. A machine shop in Houston was going to build it for me and then I'd sell it to this man in Cove, Texas.

Natalie and I were in a tight place, knowing God's going to be our provider. We were down to our last one hundred dollars—enough to cover our light bill and that's it. In a household with six kids, providing electricity is important.

We had a dilemma. I've got my own business now, twenty-four hours old, and businessmen are expected to do certain things—like taking customers to lunch.

I was trying to find a way not to spend any money. I thought, *if I can get there and it's not a meal time, maybe I can avoid spending our last hundred on lunch.*

"Just take the money and if we can hang on to it, great. Either way we'll just believe God," Natalie said.

That's my Natalie, my helpmate. Supporting me and trusting God all the way.

So off I go. I'm driving to Houston and I'm praying in tongues, but I'm pushing myself to do it. My natural man doesn't feel very joyful. But I've learned that my feelings are secondary. *The most important thing is to praise God.* So I challenge myself and in spite of my feelings, I just do it.

I'm almost to Giddings, Texas and all of a sudden, the Lord speaks to me. I know I've said sudden a lot when I've been sharing my experiences, but I can't help it. Our God really is a "suddenly" God.

Anyway, the Lord says to me, "Up ahead, there's going to be a lady, dressed all in black, sitting in the road crying. I want you to pick her up." I'm thinking *this is weird.*

But when I drive through Giddings, there she is. Dressed all in black (jeans, shirt, coat), even her hair is black. She is sitting just inside the white line that defines the right side of the road. She has her hands covering her face and she's crying. This is 290, a major highway. People just don't sit on the road here.

So I pull over and she gets up and comes right to my car.

"I'm going to Houston but I'm cutting across on the outskirts. I can give you a ride that far if you want," I said.

Without one word, she got in the car.

"God loves you," I said.

She nods her head in agreement, but she never said a word. She just kept her hands over her face and cried all the way to the outskirts of Houston.

Where Highway 290 comes in, there's a big flat field with a motel and a truck stop off to the side a little. I pull in there.

"OK. I'm going to let you out here. This is where I turn off. Maybe you can get a ride at the truck stop over there," I said.

She stopped crying, but she's still sitting there with her hands covering her face.

Then I hear the Lord say, "Give her your money." In my heart, I'm saying, *Wait a minute. That's for my children.*

But I knew that I knew that I knew that was Him. So I reached in my pocket and gave our $100 to her.

Still without one word, she takes it, opens the door, and steps out. Then she closes the door without a thank you or even a good-bye. That was it.

I started to pull out, checked for traffic, and then looked back. There's nobody there. She's gone!

This is flat land. There's no place she could have gotten to so fast. She's vanished. She's just gone.

When I get to the shop, the owner comes out to greet me with, "Can I help you?"

"I'm waiting on a part you guys are machining for me," I said.

"I know you. You do the rigs and all that stuff," he said.

"Yeah, that's me."

Right then and there he offered me a job. The salary offered was a tremendous amount. More than I'd ever made before.

[I don't want the money to take the focus off God, but He is my provider and He provides "the best" in each situation. That best for us includes money.]

"We can go ahead and we'll start this business together. You can do this and this and still get a salary. I'll put the golden handcuffs on you and you'll never want to leave," the owner said to me.

"You know, I need a top drive," he said. "Can you design a top drive?" [That's a device that goes on a drilling rig.]

"Sure."

"Great," he said, "I'll pay you extra—on top of your salary—to design the top drive for us."

The day we actually received the check was exactly ninety days from the motel incident. Our debt was totally paid off. We had a salary that was beyond belief and I was in business. Everything God told me about our finances came to pass. God is so good!

I just want to encourage everyone, when God asks you, not if, but *when* He asks you to do something that challenges you, do it. He's faithful. You won't regret it. *Let all that I am praise the Lord; may I never forget the good things he does for me* (Psalm 103:2 NLT).

7

God Heals Breast Cancer
Late 1998

*They couldn't stand the thought of food,
and they were knocking on death's door.
"Lord, help!" they cried in their trouble,
and he saved them from their distress.
He sent out his word and healed them,
snatching them from the door of death.
Let them praise the Lord for his great
love and for the wonderful things he has
done for them.*
                              —Psalm 107:18-21 NLT

A vendor, Jerry, called me and wanted to be a supplier and provide machine work for my company. Our manufacturing business was doing well, so I quickly agreed. We'd done business together before and it was all good, so we arranged to meet at his place that Tuesday.

I'd committed to drive my pastor to his church on Wednesdays, so he and his wife could ride home together instead of each of them taking their own car. I was trying to do all that I could for God. I was sure I'd be back from Jerry's in Lafayette, Louisiana in plenty of time to keep my word.

I arrived at Jerry's pretty late that Tuesday. We were having a good talk and he told me he wanted to do all our machining.

"That's good," I said.

"But, I need to tell you something," he said. "My sister-in-law is dying of breast cancer. They're going to have her funeral Friday. She's been released to hospice. My brother-in-law, Bill, set up a hospital bed in the living room so she can die at home. The funeral's Friday."

He continued, "She has breast cancer and it hit her so hard and so fast, it knocked her into a coma almost immediately. There's no hope. The family is coming in from Thailand this week. The doctor says there's no way she's going to make it." He was already broken-hearted.

It was all so sad. She was a practicing Buddhist and had no hope. What a hard situation to be in—without Jesus. We finished our dinner and went to bed.

Early the next morning, I got up ready to finalize our plans and head back to Austin. I was a man with a purpose—get that pastor to the church on time. If I left by 1 p.m. I figured I'd have just enough time to get to north Austin, pick him up, and get him to the church.

The whole time our meeting was going on, I kept watching the clock. One thing after another came up. Looking at the clock, I realized I might have to speed a little, but I'd just make it.

So I told Jerry, "We'll use your stuff." And I shot out of there.

Thirteen miles down the road on Interstate 10, the same authoritative voice I'd heard that night in the motel room asked, "Where are you going?"

God really doesn't need my answer. I already know exactly what He wants me to do.

As I spun the car around, I realized this was a person God had shown me. This is a coma—all three of the miracles He showed me were coma patients.

I called Jerry.

"God showed me I'm supposed to pray for your sister-in-law. Can I do that?" I asked.

"Let me give her husband a call and I'll call you right back," he said.

My phone rang almost immediately. "You can go," he said. "Bill told me if he didn't allow you to pray and then found out five years down the road that this stuff works, he'd never be able to live with himself." He then gave me the directions to his brother-in-law's house.

I headed over to the house, or actually it was more of a mansion. Lin's husband was a multi-millionaire, and this house was amazing.

As I pulled up I asked God, "Does she need to talk?" I knew that she was in pretty bad shape. She was dying.

"Yes, she will talk," God assured me.

I knocked and rang the doorbell for ten minutes at the front door and there was no answer. I kept knocking, determined not to leave until I did this thing for God.

"Dudley, if there was a fire in the house, could the fire department break the door down?" the Lord said.

"Yes, they could do that."

"Dudley," He told me, "there's a fire in the house!"

"Okay, Lord, in the name of Jesus," I declared. "I'm going to kick this door down."

Stepping back to do just that—the door suddenly opened. There's the brother-in-law. He turned and took off running into the house. I knew he wasn't saved because of his reaction.

He ran into a huge living room, completely empty except for Lin's hospital bed.

As I came around the corner, I was shocked to see a woman blackened by cancer. She was partially covered in a blood-soaked sheet. The amount of blood and fluids coming out of her body was terrible. The awful smell of her flesh, already decaying, permeated the room. It was more than my imagination could hold.

How can she be alive in that condition?

Death was here. I could feel it. I could see it. I could smell it. I was a bit overwhelmed by this scene, but I asked the Lord, "What am I supposed to do now that I'm here?"

"Tell the husband to repeat everything you say to his wife. It will be a two-for-one deal," the Lord said.

That sounded good to me so I told Bill to repeat what I said.

"Lin," I started.

"Lin," Bill repeats, but there's nothing.

"Lin, the Lord's here to talk to you. Come on. Let's go," I said.

I kept on speaking and he kept on repeating, but still nothing was happening.

Then Bill began crying and I was yelling inside, *"O my God, God, it's not working. She's in a coma."*

It seemed death grew even heavier in the air. This was not a game. This was Bill's hope for God to show up.

"Please, God, what do I do?"

"Dudley!" God said, "I've given you power and authority over all things. Her comatose body was a 'thing.' Stand up. Take authority over the thing. Call her to life.'"

With renewed confidence, I jumped up and with everything in me commanded, "In the name of Jesus, Lin, you open your eyes, turn your head, and repeat after me!"

She opened her eyes and looked right at me. I began a prayer of salvation. She and her husband repeated every word after me.

They were both born-again together. There was a distinct shift in the atmosphere. They had now been filled with hope. God had moved! The presence of God was in the room.

I told her Jesus wanted to heal her and asked if I could lay hands on her.

"Yes," she said.

I put my hands on each side of her face and declared, "In the name of Jesus, you are healed."

I could feel God's healing power flow into her.

All of us were crying.

The glory of God's love expelled death from that room. Only heavenly language can accurately describe what we were experiencing. Lin was awake. Awake! Her eyes were smiling.

"What do I do now?" Bill asked.

Then I heard, "clear the room." (*See Bible background for this at end of chapter.)

There was a huge four and a half foot tall golden Buddha in the corner of the living room where we were.

"That's got to go." I told him.

I was thinking they'd probably remove it in a week or so. Not so. Bill charged over to the sliding glass doors, flung them all the way open, grabbed that Buddha, and hurled it out the doors. It landed on the marble tile and was smashed to smithereens.

I thought, *Wow, Buddha's airborne, he's not messing around!*

He never hesitated. Bill asked, "What next?"

I began to point to the idols around the room. Everything I pointed to became missiles flying out the door. One after another, whenever I said, "That needs to go," he made sure it was out of there.

When all the symbols of those false gods were destroyed, Bill asked again, "What now?"

Then the Holy Spirit gave these instructions to me and I told them: "No one is to enter Lin's room unless they can confess, 'Jesus Christ is Lord and He reigns in my life.' If they can't say it, they can't come in."

> *By this you know the Spirit of God: Every spirit that confesses that Jesus Christ has come in the flesh is of God, and every*

spirit that does not confess Jesus Christ has come in the flesh is not of God.
                    —1 John 4:2-3 NKJV

"But her parents are coming for the funeral," Bill said.

"Bill," I said, looking right at him, "There's not going to be any funeral. But if they can't say this, don't let them in the room."

"But Dudley, the Catholic priest is coming to give her the last rites."

"Bill, there is not going to be any last rites. I am serious. Nobody gets into this room unless they declare Jesus is Lord."

"What do they need to say?" he asked.

I wrote it down for him.

"Right," he says, "I got it. If they don't say it, they are not coming into this room."

With that settled, I turned to go and he hugged me all the way to the car. I don't know how, maybe I was transported or what, but I made that trip back to Austin in time to pick up the pastor.

There was no way in the natural I could have driven that fast. But because I'd made that promise to pastor, God moved on my behalf to make my words true. My word is very important to me. What I say, I do.

As soon as I got out of church that evening, I turned my cell phone on and Bill called.

"Lin made me put her in a wheelchair and take her outside. I've been wheeling her back and forth, up and down the whole street. She's so happy she won't let me take her inside."

"Give the phone to Lin," I said.

"Lin, take it easy. Go back inside. Get your rest. God is with you," I said.

The next morning, Bill called again and told me that Lin was sitting at the kitchen table eating breakfast.

"That's cool," I said.

"No, you don't understand, she has been on a feeding tube since she went into a coma."

Within two weeks, she was totally healed. All her family and many others came to the Lord. She went from church to church to church giving her testimony.

We kept in touch. I sent Bill books and recordings about God and His works. It was such a blessing to hear almost daily of her walk with God. Then one day Bill called.

"Lin went home to be with the Lord. She is up there cooking for him, she loved to cook."

"I'm so sorry." I was stunned.

"No, Dudley," Bill said. "You don't understand. When she was sick, the coma hit so fast, we didn't get to say good-bye or anything. But that last night, Lin told me, 'God's taking me home tonight.' And He did. We had an autopsy and there was no sign of cancer or anything else that could have caused her death. God just took her home."

It was exactly nine months to the very day I had prayed for her.

> *Precious (important and no light matter) in the sight of the Lord is the death of His saints (His loving ones).*
> —Psalm 116:15 AMP

> *Idols are worthless; they are ridiculous lies! On the day of reckoning they will all be destroyed.*
> —Jeremiah 51:18 NLT

*Accursed things.
God said, "The graven images of their gods you shall burn with fire. You shall not desire the silver or gold that is on them, nor take it for yourselves, lest you be ensnared by it, for it is an abomination to the LORD your God. Neither shall you bring an abomination (an idol) into your house, lest you become an accursed thing like it; but you shall utterly detest and abhor it, for it is an accursed thing.
> —Deuteronomy 7:25-26 AMP

8

God Heals Brain Hemorrhage
September 1999

*At that very time, Jesus cured many
people of their diseases, illnesses, and
evil spirits, and he restored sight to many
who were blind.*

—Luke 7:21 NLT

Natalie and I found ourselves in another new season. Because of the downturn in the oil business, we had to close the Austin office and work out of Houston. The company I was working for had a guest house, so I stayed there Monday through Friday and then drove home to Austin on weekends.

On work week evenings, I'd go into town to eat. Natalie would bless me saying, "You can go to the International House of Pancakes (IHOP) once or twice a week, but that's all." She always watches out for my diet. She wants me to stay healthy.

Every time I went into IHOP, the Lord would say, "Go talk to this one."

He showed me people to share His love with. So many people started coming to the Lord, the management began giving me free meals. That's really a demonstration of God's favor since the owners were Muslim.

✝

In my spare time, I'd go to the malls or anywhere I sensed God leading me.

My life was not my own any more. I "died to self" that September 16 in the motel room and Jesus is alive and living in me. It is quite an adventure.

✝

One day, I was in the company parking lot talking to the Lord. It had been about a week since anything major had happened, so I said, "Lord, you haven't used me in a long time."

To me, seven days was a long time.

Then my beeper went off. It was the church we were attending in Austin.

"A woman from our church is away at a women's conference. She has just been notified by the hospital that her father has a brain hemorrhage and they want to perform surgery.

She's very concerned because he isn't saved and she doesn't want to give permission for the procedure until you go talk to him. Will you go?"

"Sure," I said, thinking *that was fast, Lord.*

He was right there in Houston. Immediately, I start for the hospital.

"No. I didn't tell you to go yet. I will tell you when to go." I heard the Lord say.

"This man is in serious condition. This is urgent." I'm reasoning with the Lord. *Like He doesn't know everything there is to know about everything. But I know it's more important to do this God's way than to run in there on my own. So I wait.*

I'd been waiting for almost two hours when I said, "Lord, I'm not going to the hospital, I'm just running to the store for a Coke."

So I'm getting ready to make a right-hand turn for the store when the Lord says, "Turn left."

So I have a little pity party. "I waited and waited, two and a half hours. Now, when I want to get a Coke you say GO. Unbelievable, but I'm going."

I didn't really know the way. I just began driving and the Lord told me every single turn along the way and got me to the hospital.

At the front desk, they didn't want to let me in. "Are you a minister?" they asked.

Our pastor just preached that we are all ministers of reconciliation (2 Cor. 5:18), so I am a minister, I thought.

I looked at him and said, "Yes."

"Are you family?" the receptionist asked, shaking his head.

"Yes, he's my brother," I answered. *I've always heard Christians saying things like, he's my brother, and we're all members of the family of God.*

He just shook his head again and said, "Go on in."

When I went into his room, there were lots and lots of tiny x-rays on this white board. He was in a medically induced coma because his daughter hadn't given consent for the surgery. There were two doctors and several nurses attending to him, adjusting IV's, and checking vital signs.

"Hello. I need to talk to David," I said.

"He's not doing any talking. He's unresponsive," the doctor said.

"I understand," I told him. "But this is real important so he's going to talk."

Then I looked directly at David and said, "David, open your eyes. Jesus sent me here to tell you He loves you."

David turned his head and opened his eyes.

Now we have every one's attention, even the

nurses' station. Everyone became completely still and quiet.

"David, Jesus wants me to tell you that He loves you. And He wants me to make sure that if anything happens to you, you'll be with Him for eternity."

"Okay, answer me this one question first. Is there a heaven?" he asked.

I found out later that David had always fought Christianity and especially heaven.

I didn't know heaven was his problem, but God did, so the answer I gave was, "I don't know what we would call it, but I'd think any-where Jesus is—that's heaven."

He agreed with that so I said, "Let's make sure Jesus is your Lord and Savior."

He took my hand and I began to lead him in a three steps to salvation kind of prayer. When I said, "Repeat after me"—not only David repeated the prayer, the doctors and nurses were repeating the prayer too! That was something else. God is so good! But there's more!

Then I told David, "Jesus wants to heal you. Can I pray for you?"

"Yes," He answered. But all the doctors are answering for him and they're saying yes too.

I put my hand on his head and said in a normal tone, "In the name of Jesus, you are healed."

"Is that it?" David asked.

"That's it," I tell him and start walking out of the room. "We'll have to go to lunch sometime."

I drove all the way back to the guest house and arrived around 4:30 p.m.

I get a call from David's daughter. Because of the delay caused by waiting for prayer, they had to retake all the x-rays. When they got the x-rays back, all evidence of the hemorrhaged blood was completely gone.

David was released from the hospital— totally healed!

"Thank You, Jesus!"

When I was in the motel room in that God sphere, He showed me three key people that I would pray for. I never saw their faces, just their symptoms. David was another one of those people.

9

Healings in ICU
October 1999

I call heaven and earth as witnesses today against you, that I have set before you life and death, blessing and cursing; therefore choose life, that both you and your descendants may live; that you may love the LORD your God, that you may obey His voice, and that you may cling to Him, for He is your life and the length of your days.
—Deuteronomy 30:19-20 NKJV

David's testimony quickly spread through the church. The very *next* day, I got another call from the church. Someone had a sister in Hospice Emergency with complete kidney failure due to substance abuse. The doctor had said her kidneys were dead.

From the symptoms, I realized this is another of the miracles God told me about in the sphere.

When I arrive, I find they have a high level of security. Police and security guards are everywhere. They even have me go through metal detectors and ask me if I have any weapons.

"All I have is the Word of God, the Bible, and it is a two-edged sword," I said.

They didn't think that was very funny, and they had me put the Bible through the x-ray.

At the ICU entrance, the doctor ran me off saying there was no way I could see her. "This area is restricted. You must have family permission to see her, even if you're a pastor."

No wonder there were so many police: The ICU was treating addicts and criminals!

"What do I do now, Lord?" I asked as I went out the swinging glass doors. On my left was a waiting area.

"Hide," He said.

As odd as this sounded, I hid behind a soda machine and waited.

The doctor soon left with an armful of folders. I saw my chance and went back in.

The ICU was arranged in a circle. There were only curtains separating the patients. Not much privacy. The nurse's station was in the center, allowing the staff to keep an eye on everything and everyone.

This woman's last name was unusual so when I found the board with the name written in marker, I knew I was in the right place and went in.

Her bed faced the nurse's station. Two other nurses were there drawing blood and checking vital signs. Susan's eyes were closed. She was motionless.

Carrying my Bible, I went in and said, "Susan."

There was no response.

A voice from the nurses' station in the center said, "She's not going to hear you, she is in a coma."

"She is?" I asked.

"She is."

Then I said, "Susan, look at me. I'm here to tell you God loves you. He sent me here to tell you that."

Susan turned her head, opened her eyes, and looked right at me.

Immediately, a complete silence came over the entire ICU. There was no privacy, so the minute she opened her eyes, everyone, including the patients in the ward, was watching us to see what would happen next.

God definitely had their attention. I spoke loud enough for everyone to hear.

"Susan, I'm here to tell you Jesus loves you and if something happens, He wants you to be

89

with Him for eternity. Let's pray and take care of that."

"Yes," she said and reached for my hand. We held hands and I asked her to repeat after me.

"Jesus," I started. Her voice was joined by an entire chorus of voices—nurses, patients, everyone throughout the hospital ICU declaring "Jesus" in unison.

With their very own eyes, they had just seen the miracle of Susan awakening from the coma. Our God moves in mighty ways.

After we prayed the prayer of salvation, I told her, "God wants to heal you, but He won't put anything on you without being invited. He wants you to ask Him."

She nodded and said, "Yes, please."

Then I put my hand on her head and said, "Susan, in the name of Jesus, you are healed."

"Is that it?" she asked, as I started to leave.

"That's it. Jesus loves you," I said. Then I left.

I knew I needed to leave quickly before the doctor returned. To ignore the hospital rules was outside of my comfort zone. All of this happened on Wednesday.

Her brother called to let me know Susan was released on Thursday. Her kidney function was totally restored.

By Friday evening, every single person that had been in that ICU wing was healed and released. Jesus and I, we emptied out the ICU!

✝

God loves people. All kinds of people. When the Apostle Paul was in a ship filled with prisoners headed for Rome, he gave them God's warning not to sail on. But they did anyway and were caught in such a huge storm, even the seasoned sailors were afraid.

Then an angel told Paul, *"Do not be afraid ... God has granted you all those who sail with you"* (Acts 27:24, author paraphrased).

Some jumped overboard when they thought it was shallow enough for them to make it on their own. But all who stayed on-board with Paul, and trusted God, were saved. Prisoners and soldiers, not the elite of society, all 276 of them were saved because God loves and cares about each and every one of us.

Before Calvary, Jesus and His twelve disciples were the only ones doing most of God's healing work. But when Jesus rose again, He sent us His Holy Spirit.

Just before He was crucified, Jesus said:

However, I am telling you nothing but the truth when I say it is profitable (good, expedient, advantageous) for you that I go away. Because if I do not go away, the Comforter (Counselor, Helper, Advocate, Intercessor, Strengthener, and Standby) will not come to you [into close fellowship with you]: but if I go away, I will send Him to you [to be in close fellowship with you].

—John 16:7 AMP

When more of us share His love, His healing, and His forgiveness, it releases those who receive His touch to praise Him.

When they share what they've received, more people come to know Him, love Him, and praise Him.

They share His love and more and more the number of healings grows. More people are saved and even more are praising God.

We find we are seeing the greater works, greater numbers, greater everything! God is so good!

10

Mission to Mexico
March 2008

May God, who gives this patience and encouragement, help you live in complete harmony with each other, as is fitting for followers of Christ Jesus. Then all of you can join together with one voice, giving praise and glory to God, the Father of our Lord Jesus Christ.
—Romans 15:5-6 NLT

God opened the door for Natalie and I to be part of a short-term mission team going to the mid-size city Acámboro in Mexico. There were no tourists here. Natalie really wanted to go, but this was going to be a stretch for me. I was right at home in Houston and Austin, but Mexico? Different language, different food, and different customs. God was taking me out of my comfort zone.

I told God I really wanted to see a miracle on this trip and I was willing to do whatever it took. Then I promised Him I wouldn't complain about anything—not food, not accommodations, nothing. There were no four star hotels where we were going. The stars were gone, but still I wasn't going to complain.

The entire team decided we'd just use our first names. We wanted to be almost incognito, hiding in His glory.

We stopped on the way for some authentic Mexican tacos. They make them with a little meat and about fifty pounds of onions. At that time I had such a sensitive stomach, just the smell of onions could give me big trouble. And they did. I had to fight to keep it together the entire bus ride.

Getting to our room was a relief, but the plumbing was outdated, releasing the sewage smell into the room. Not good. I have to admit it was hard not to complain, but I wanted to see God do a miracle so I kept quiet.

After we got settled in our room, we went over to check the venue that had been rented for the pastor's conference. The space was about 60 x 80 feet square with a tile floor and double glass doors. We all sensed a dark heaviness inside. We learned that the previous week a witch's conference had been held in this area.

We started to set up folding chairs and pray for the conference. I heard the Lord say, "Lay down flat on the floor."

I'm a real guy so that's not something I would ever do. I'm just setting up chairs, and God's already messing with my comfort zone. But I went ahead and did it.

That broke something off me—I'd humbled myself. Even after all the amazing miracles I'd seen God do, that simple act of obedience changed me.

We were a group, not individuals, linked even closer than a family by the bond of the Spirit.

The pastors of the town all came together to build unity and tear down a wall of competition that separated them. It was a beautiful thing to see. They had stopped comparing themselves one to another and were just happy to worship our Lord together.

In my own eyes, I was the least qualified in our group to do anything. I had no formal education in the things of God. Yet, here we were to tell people about God. Deep down, I knew it was important that I was there. This was a time for me to enjoy the relationships God was building, the deeper link of the Spirit we all shared, and be joined together for His purpose. Everything was to glorify God. For

Natalie and me to experience all of this together as a couple was priceless.

When the ministry time began, a woman pastor was slain in the Spirit and fell to the ground. I immediately thought I needed to stand behind the people to catch them when they fell. The floor was cement. (God's divine love seems to overwhelm them and they simply fall down.)

Angela, a prophet from Venezuela, and other prophets from our team started spinning in a prophetic action. From the back where I stood, a whirlwind of God appeared to fill the front of the room. As it began to blow, enlarge, and touch people, some flew backward horizontally in the air.

At this point I thought, *Can't catch them now, they are on their own!* The power of God was definitely there. We were literally all blown away by this event.

This demonstration, this sign, unlocked the hearts of the pastors. They were wide-open to God and all He had for them. Their commitment to work together for God created a safe place for those who were saved during the conference to continue to grow in Jesus.

Many of us went out into the streets passing out flyers advertising the meeting we were having. About 400 came. Praise God!

At the very beginning, each couple from our team stood to be introduced. Natalie and I stood. I did not want to be lifted up.

I said, "Lord, I present to You the people of Acámbaro."

A woman with us was taking our picture at that exact moment. She told us she saw a flash over my head. When we saw the picture, we could see the flash and a shadowed outline of an angel standing behind me. Out of all the pictures she took that night, mine is the only one where the flash and angelic figure appeared.

When the invitation to receive prayer was given, people started coming forward from all over the room. The woman leading us turned to me and said, "This one's yours."

> *"Please ask the Lord Your God to restore my hand again!"*
> —1 Kings 13:6 NLT

I saw a little boy, Carlos, with a withered arm that was badly curled up. He was the first one to come for prayer. I was wishing he had a headache or something easier to start with. But

97

it's all easy for God. I didn't really know what I was doing (as usual).

"God, either you're going to look really good here or really bad. So, what do I do?" I said.

Clear as a bell, the Holy Spirit began to guide me saying, "Everything I've given you, give to that boy. Put your hand on the elbow of his withered arm, and then drag your hand along his arm out to his hand."

As I did exactly that, drawing my hand down his arm, his arm began to expand, just like one of those long balloons clowns twist into animal shapes for children. His arm filled out with new muscle all the way to his fingers. He turned to face the crowd, lifted his arms, uncurled his hands, and started praising God with two perfect arms.

When the crowd saw this miracle, they went crazy. There was glorious chaos as everyone started praying for people and people were being healed all over the place.

The next one I prayed for was a woman, who was deaf in one ear, the interpreter told me. With little Carlos still clinging to my leg, I said, "Lord, I give this woman everything you have given me."

I actually "felt" a popping in her ear. I felt God's healing power flowing out of me and into her. It left me totally drained with no energy at all. She was completely healed.

When I turned to the next one, God doubled the energy of the healing power He'd given me with the first one. I could feel "healing mittens" on my hands. (This is a sign God sometimes gives me for healing. With some people, their hands get warm or tingly. I get mittens that go all the way up to my elbows.)

The next person I prayed for was a lady with her tongue hanging outside her mouth. It was so swollen, the size of an apple, it couldn't fit in her mouth. Her tongue was cracked with sores all over.

I prayed for her that same way, giving her everything Jesus had given me and declaring, "You are healed in the Name of Jesus."

Again, I felt His healing touch leave me and flow into her. Immediately, her tongue popped back into her mouth. She lifted her hands and began praising God in Spanish.

Next, two boys came up together. One of them wore thick glasses that looked like coke bottles. Through the interpreter, I found out he couldn't see very far. I was learning, so I put my fingers on his eyes and gave him everything Jesus had given me.

We had some posters on the wall, and now he could read them. Thank you, Jesus! He could see!

Without any warning, a woman towards the back of the crowd fell down. I heard, *"la muerte, la muerte!"* shouted out.

That means "dead" in Spanish. Natalie and I made a beeline for her, me from one side, Nat from the other side. I put my hand on her neck and there was no pulse. As soon as I touched her, a picture flashed in my mind of bluish and whitish O-rings.

Then the Lord said, "That's the valves in her heart. They're closed. Pray that My Blood will flow through there and I will open them up."

Natalie was on the other side of her praying, while I prayed as the Lord had directed me.

Immediately, the woman jumped up, lifting her hands, and praising God.

I had asked God to let me see a miracle and He allowed me to see so many—all the miracles in the Bible, I saw.

Jesus said:
> *The blind see and the lame walk; the lepers are cleansed and the deaf hear; the dead are raised up and the poor have the gospel preached to them.*
> —Matthew 11:5 NKJV

I even saw creative miracles as I watched Carlos' arm made whole. I will never forget little Carlos!

I prayed for one girl who had an extra bone in her hand. I actually felt it. It left and she was healed.

All of us were seeing God do so much, much more than He could have accomplished with just one person. The "unity" and the power of God displayed there was beyond anything I'd ever witnessed before. I'd seen miracles, just me and Jesus, but this was so much greater. So much more. I was in awe of what God could do with a group united and committed to doing His will.

When this was over, Natalie suggested that our group pray for me. I was still battling severe stomach issues. I'd traveled with big packs of antacids handy since I was a young man.

They gathered around me and prayed. Then when the leader of our team laid hands on me, I went down under the power of God. I felt my stomach untwisting. The pain was finally gone. Thank you, God!

There's a reward when we follow Him, when we pray for others, our healing is there. But He releases blessings and healings for us much faster as we pray for others. I wasn't worried about my need or discomfort. But God loves me and He wanted me healed too.

That night after the meeting, we went for some of those famous Mexican tacos packed with onions. I had six or seven with no problems at all. I was totally healed.

The next day, our team divided into small groups to minister at churches and home churches where we'd been invited. Everybody walks a lot there. There aren't many cars, so Natalie and I walked with the pastor to his church.

"I had a dream and I was wondering if you can interpret it for me?" the pastor said.

After he told me the dream, I paused a moment and asked the Lord, "What does this mean?" Then God gave me the interpretation which I gave to the pastor.

"That's right on," he said. "That's what God showed me, too." I don't know if it was confirmation or a test. I only know that we encouraged him. When Natalie and I shared God's love with his home church, it was great, just the two of us pouring out God's tender love on His people.

We were wrapping up our time in Mexico, so one of the sisters wanted to prepare a lunch for all of us. They were so hospitable, so warm. Our wives took a cab and although it was a long walk with some steep hills, we guys felt we were up for walking through town.

We'd kind of been joking around that we were tough enough to walk and keep up with the local guys.

When we reached the town square, we heard all kinds of shouting and yelling. There was a big crowd watching a knife fight.

One guy had a ten-inch knife and he'd been hit on the head. The other guy had a pipe and he had a knife wound. The crowd went silent as they opened up and let us through.

We definitely didn't belong, but I went up to the guy with the knife. I put my hand on his chest. I don't know Spanish, but I said, "Jesus, amour."

We brought God's peace into the atmosphere. He dropped the knife to his side. The other guy dropped the pipe. There were three of us there. The other men in our group were with the guy who'd had the pipe. And they were talking to him. I didn't understand them, but I knew they were speaking the peace of God's love into this man.

Then the man who had the knife in his hand walked around behind me. That unnerved me, but God said, "Trust me. Don't turn around."

He continued walking back around in front of us, dropped his knife, and then each man went his way. We walked out the other side of the crowd and down the road.

We all saw God's peace take over that square. We are peacemakers. We walked into a bad situation and established God's love and peace there.

The trip changed me in so many ways. But to hear God say, "Thank you," well, how can you find the words to describe what that does to your heart?

Well done, good and faithful servant.
—Matthew 25:21 NKJV

As each one has received a gift, minister it to one another, as good stewards of the manifold grace of God. If anyone speaks, let him speak as the oracles of God. If anyone ministers, let him do it as with the ability which God supplies, that in all things God may be glorified through Jesus Christ, to whom belong the glory and the dominion forever and ever. Amen.
—1 Peter 4:10-11 NKJV

11

Lakeland Revival
May 2008

I tell you the truth, anyone who believes in me will do the same works I have done, and even greater works, because I am going to be with the Father. You can ask for anything in my name, and I will do it, so that the Son can bring glory to the Father. Yes, ask me for anything in my name, and I will do it.

—John 14:12-14 NLT

Natalie: One of my friends shared with me about the revival going on in Lakeland, Florida. Just hearing about what God was doing there made me hunger for more of Him.

I asked, "Can I go, Lord?" In my heart, I heard a resounding "yes."

We were looking for a new church home and this transition time was hard. In some ways, we were drained and worn out. That's what a performance-based walk does to you.

I asked Dudley and my children if they wanted to go and no one really wanted to. Dudley said he would go because he loves me.

I began to watch the Lakeland live broadcasts on my computer. The more I saw, the more I wanted to be there. Our son, Nathan, watched in his bedroom. He said God demonstrated His power and knocked him back a couple of feet right there in his bedroom. So he wanted to go. That made three of us.

Dudley: I had a fear-of-man thing nagging at me. If I took a week off work, maybe they'd decide they didn't really need me. But I'd heard about another move of God that I missed out on and I didn't want to miss out on what God was doing in Lakeland too.

So I drove six hours home from working in Odessa. Immediately, the three of us jumped in the car and drove non-stop for twenty-two hours to the revival in Florida.

We rotated driving and arrived at the airport location where the meetings were being held. We were late and the only available seats were towards the back. They had brought in folding chairs and we sat out in the open air. This was before they moved to the tent. It was a bit like Woodstock back in 1969.

We could see the preacher on the platform, but more importantly, everybody was praying for everybody. The freedom of the Spirit among us was incredible.

We looked up. In the sky behind us, there was a cloud formation in the shape of a cross. In the sky towards the front, there was a cloud formation of a dove.

People were pointing to them and praising God. All through the audience there were shouts of joy as miracle after miracle was taking place. The freedom was exciting.

> *Now the Lord is the Spirit, and where the Spirit of the Lord is, there is liberty (emancipation from bondage, freedom).*
> —2 Corinthians 3:17 AMP

Instead of us watching God flowing only through the leaders on the platform, we were watching what God was doing through the believers in the audience. It was wonderful and wild!

I raised my hands in praise to Him. We were immersed in a rushing river of God's love. Suddenly, I felt like fire was coming from my left hand.

"Natalie, there's fire in my left hand," I said.

From the platform the evangelist says, "God has just put a coal of fire in somebody's left hand." The presence of God was so strong.

Natalie and I joined some other believers and prayed for a woman in a wheelchair. She was healed and got up and walked.

People were shouting, "JESUS! JESUS!"

Healings and miracles were happening all over in this mob of God's glory. It was so exciting, you didn't want to leave. We went home changed. God breathed His life into us and we were all changed.

> *And the Word became flesh and dwelt among us, and we beheld His glory.*
> —John 1:14 NKJV

Nathan came home renewed and running after God. We knew this wasn't just for us. We needed to take others. So we filled a van and car with friends and several of our children to go with us on our second trip. We had to drive our car to have room for Natalie and I. It was Mother's Day and the meetings had grown so much they were being held in the Coliseum. It was the same joy. The same love. The same liberty. It was really Jesus.

Someone gave me a "Jesus is Lord" baseball cap. I'm not much of a hat person, but the Lord told me to accept it, but not wear it. God cares about the little stuff. Even the hairs on our head are numbered (Matthew 10:30 NKJV).

Later that day, we went to lunch. The Lord spoke to me to get the hat. An older English couple approached us and asked where I got that hat. I knew I needed to give it to him. He hugged me and wept with joy.

That night, the speaker called that same couple out of the crowd and told them revival was going to break out in his church and go all over England. This confirmed God wanted him to have that hat. Simple things can show others the many signs of His glorious love.

One night they had us line up to have the preacher lay hands on us. With ten thousand people, that was going to take a while.

I prayed, "Lord, touch your people."

When I said that, I felt electricity fly out of one of my fingers. I had injured it badly twenty years earlier. The damaged nerves and tissue had been removed and I had no feeling in it. As we walked out across the parking lot, I ran my hand against a car. I could "feel" it in that finger that had been injured. God created new nerves in that finger of mine!

When I wrote the sponsoring ministry to share what God had done, they replied, "Isn't it funny, you asked God to touch His people and it takes feeling to touch somebody." God is so amazing.

The next morning, we all attended a ministry equipping and releasing class. It started with worship and God said, "Give it everything you've got."

He must have said it to all of us, in unity we all charged after God, praising Him, and holding nothing back. We now had our family on fire, pressing in as one body in praise and purpose.

The leader said, "You guys don't need me to teach you. You're doing it! Go for it!"

> *And the Lord will create over the whole site, over every dwelling place of Mt. Zion and over her assemblies, a cloud and smoke by day and the shining of a flaming fire by night, for over all the glory shall be a canopy (a defense of divine love and protection).*
>
> —Isaiah 4:5 AMP

Praise while worshipping is the key to entering into God's glory. He brings us in and we are in the atmosphere of eternity.

When we started to praise God in the evening meeting, we were immediately back in that heavenly state as if our praise had continued uninterrupted. Praise and worship exploded. We were praising Him with all our heart and strength. Suddenly, twenty octaves of heavenly voices joined us, singing notes impossible for any of us.

We fell to our knees. The worship leader was on his hands and knees prostrate before the King of Glory. It was loud, it was majestic. The heavenly choir sang with us for about twenty minutes. The angels joined us. It was Heaven on earth. We praised until the Spirit released us in the glory, the heavenly realm of eternity.

We were declaring "great and mighty is the Lord God Almighty" and the angels came and joined in. This was another touchstone experience for me.

I knew that when things in life get confusing I will always remember the night the angels came, not to a motel room, but to join with us in praise to our Almighty God.

On our way home, I really wanted to go to the beach, so Natalie and I decided to spend an extra night and leave the next morning. Six a.m. is my idea of morning. Natalie was a good sport and went with me. She wanted to lie in the sand while I splashed around in the water.

As I walked into the water, I started singing "Jesus, Lord of All" at the top of my lungs. I'm no singer, but no one else was on the beach so

I just kept singing away to the Lord. When I was about waist deep, I looked down and saw a big shark—right there!

I dashed out of there so fast. Usually that would have been the end of me and the water. I told Nat about the shark, but she was half asleep. She just mumbled, "Uh huh."

So I went back in and this time I got stung by jelly fish. I went back to tell Natalie.

"Rub some sand on it," she said.

So I go back in again still singing, "Jesus, Lord of all," but now I'm really concentrating on the water around me. Some little fishes started coming. The more I sang to the Lord, the more they came, as if they were my audience. More jelly fish came and I ended up getting stung five more times. I was popping in and out of the ocean water and onto the beach.

I'd better turn this song off. It's attracting all these fish and jelly fish, I thought.

Then I heard the Lord say, "Dudley, the light in you will draw many to you, even the ones you do not want. You're going to get stung, but keep pressing forward. Keep pressing in."

God is preparing us for something big. Intimacy with Him is the only way to get ready.

Loving Him, under His wings, is the only place of protection.

> *Because he has set his love upon Me, therefore I will deliver him; I will set him on high, because he has known My name, [has a personal knowledge of My mercy, love, and kindness—trusts and relies on Me, knowing I will never forsake him, no never].*
> —Psalm 91:14 AMP

The third time we went to Lakeland Revival, I heard God say, "Free my people." I knew this was *my* assignment.

The first restraint to be broken is the "traditions of man" that limit us. It's when people say: "Things should only be done this way," or "Get someone important to pray for me."

I was realizing God wants to free us from our old ways. He wants us to ask Him to show us His higher way. His ways are better than ours. Much better!

Next meeting, God dealt with the "religious spirit" that stifles revival. People were freed to grow in the Spirit and be led by the Holy Spirit. Chains of control were shattered and many were set free.

12

Amazing Asia
May 2010

If any of you lacks wisdom, let him ask of
God, who gives to all liberally and without
reproach, and it will be given to him. But
let him ask in faith, with no doubting, for
he who doubts is like a wave of the sea
driven and tossed by the wind.
—James 1:5-6 NKJV

In this season of my life, I sold some technology to Asia. God gives me ideas of how to put things together, new ways, and new ideas. He gives me designs, step-by-step.

God tells me, "Do this," and I do. I did one big unit in thirteen days working twenty-two hours a day. That's not possible in the natural, but He gave me the energy and clarity plus the ability. I knew I could depend on God.

When I completed one phase, I could sense His excitement as if He could hardly wait for me to get to the stage when I could ask Him, "What next, Lord?"

He gave me designs that we sent for third party analysis on a big rig. This company did the finite analysis programs, testing strengths and load factors, and running computer programs to make sure the design met all the standards of the oil industry. They told me that for the first time in the thirty-two years they'd been in business, there were no errors and nothing needed to be changed.

God knows how to design equipment.

✝

The negotiations with the company finally came to the point when they said, "Now's the time." That meant I was off to Asia.

I was so unconcerned. I didn't even research the city I was going to. This trip was very different for me. I had no anxiety about the new situation I was going into. I wasn't worried about connections or new airports or anything. I knew I was with God and He had everything under control.

They sent a limousine to pick me up.

Do you know who you're here for? Dudley? I'm just plain old Dudley.

God poured His favor over me and they took me to a really nice hotel. They treated me like a

116

king, insisting on paying all my expenses. I wasn't used to that, but I appreciated it.

On our first meeting, I presented them with the memory sticks containing the computer programs, different drawings, and other data.

They decided to have their engineers go over it the next day. Then we could go through any questions they had. We would start our meeting the following day.

The president of the company and their chief engineer were at this initial meeting. They had two interpreters as a precaution to maintain accuracy and to make sure nothing was missed or misunderstood.

I realized I didn't have the invoice which we needed to establish a line of credit. They volunteered to make one for me. This was so easy. They were doing all the work for me.

God was way ahead of me preparing the way with all the help I needed. A government official also attended this meeting. It is customary there for government and business to be partnered. A decision was made to meet at an auditorium to film everything that was said. I'm not sure why we needed to film it, but that's how we did it.

The next morning I woke up at 4:30 a.m. I opened the blinds to a picture postcard scene. The sun was up and the view from the twelfth floor was picturesque. A beautiful river was flowing in the distance. People were sweeping the streets. It was a charming scene.

I was praising and worshipping God, nothing structured, just spontaneously thanking Him for all He is and all He had done. I remembered how I presented to God the people in Mexico. So I said, "Lord, I present to You the people of this nation."

There was an immediate shift in the atmosphere of my room. The glory of the Lord came in. The presence of God was so heavy, I knew something different was going on. I didn't know what, but I knew something was about to happen.

They arranged for me to go on a sightseeing tour that day while their engineers went over my data.

"God, I'm going to take you with me wherever I go today," I said.

The limo picked me up around 8:00 a.m. The two interpreters were there to show me around. They understood English, so on the way I shared about God's love with them. I didn't shove Jesus down their throats, I just loved on them.

When I got in the back seat of the limo, I could feel the hairs on Jesus' arm brush against my arm. No one was sitting next to me, but I could feel His arm.

We were really going together! Wow!

118

We got there and I stepped out of the limo. It felt like Jesus was shadow-walking with me. When I took a step to the right, I could feel His foot right next to mine. When I stepped to the left, the same thing happened.

The next step I took to the right felt like I stepped into Jesus. I was surrounded by Him. I could feel His heart beat, His love. When I leaned back a bit, it was like I leaned against His chest. I could feel His heart beating. His love surrounded me, like I was inside a cocoon of God's Love.

About sixty yards away, an old man looked up at me. Then he starts in a full-blown run right to me. As fast as he could, he hugs me, wraps his arms around me, puts his head on my chest, and starts crying for joy.

I could just feel the love pouring out of God's heart through my head right into this man. I could feel God's tears. I could feel God's love for him. I could feel this man's love for God.

We were both in the glory of God's love and we didn't say a word. We didn't need to. It was beyond words. Other people came running and it was the same thing. They would come up and hug me and I could just feel God's intense love for each of them. The interpreters watched all this going on with smiles.

It was raining so the interpreters went to get umbrellas. They treated me like royalty. We walked along this grey marble wall. It stood seven to eight feet tall. We were about five feet away from it just walking. People began pointing at me. On the wall where my shadow should have been, there was a dry silhouette of a man bigger than me.

The people were saying, "You're hot. You're drying out the wall." The dry silhouette followed me and the previous spot would become wet with the rain. That wasn't me doing that, it was Jesus. And more and more people came up hugging me.

The interpreters told me this was very strange behavior. They aren't a demonstrative culture. When they hugged me, they were really hugging Jesus and He loved on them through me. There were armed guards watching everything, on alert. I didn't say anything about Jesus. I just loved them.

This went on all day. And when we reached the square, there were tables and booths selling souvenirs and such. One woman had a booth of idols. She had a 1-inch square stick about a yard long she used to point at each different one as she shouted the prices. We got closer, about five feet away, and the stick she was holding straight out snapped in two pieces.

She screamed and put her arms up, When she looked up towards heaven the tears came. I knew and she knew and God knew that she had encountered the King of Kings.

✝

So they brought the sick out into the streets and laid them on beds and couches, that at least the shadow of Peter passing by might fall on some of them. And a multitude gathered from the surrounding cities to Jerusalem, bringing sick people and those tormented by unclean spirits, and they were all healed.

—Acts 5:15-16 NKJV

The Lord said to me, "If my people will take me places, they will walk in me, just as you are doing now. In the Bible when people were healed by Peter's shadow, he was walking in me as you are today. If my people will take me with them, I will pay the bill."

It reminded me of when a father takes his child to lunch. The father pays the bill. It's an honor to walk in Jesus.

The next day the company began to film everything for documentation, for national television, and even for commercials. God's glory released a calmness and comfort over everyone. His favor seemed to be all over the place.

They told me they'd decided six months after our negations started to go ahead with this project. They had the funding there and everything was ready to go. But they wanted to wait to see if I would change.

Isn't that just like God, I thought. *Here everything I wanted was ready to go, but the delay proved I was serious. I was authentic.*

The business aspects of this deal just went like clockwork. Although it isn't my normal routine, every day I wore a tie because God said that since I was representing Him, I should. I was always loving to everyone I met. I never played the big shot role. I just kept telling them we're all the same. That was hard for them to take hold of.

I would be asked by the vice-presidents and other important people, "How did you come up with these designs?"

I'd say, "God is good," giving Him all the credit.

"But how?" They'd ask.

"God just shows me things and I copy them," I answered.

There was a gaming table there—a type of "dominoes" with characters on one side that numbered one to ten.

"Let's see how good you are."

They wanted to test me. So they took the dominoes and mixed them all up. Then they wanted me to guess the character on the other side. I got them all right. So they mixed them again and I got them all right again.

God is good.

My last morning there, the limo picked me up and took me to the company, which was like a city in itself. When I arrived, I was stunned to see everyone standing outside to greet me, over 7,600 people. And they were all wearing a tie to show respect to me. When the president arrived at work, he saw everyone with a tie and he went out and bought one too.

I knew I had represented Jesus well when the president told me in over thirty years of dealing with Americans, I was the most honest person they had ever met.

They wanted to honor me, so they had a committee that met for three days to decide the perfect thing to give me. I was presented with a crystal bell on a stand as a very special gift.

"We didn't want to get you something ordinary because you aren't ordinary," the president told me. "This bell is a replica of a bell up in the mountains that the monks toll every day. The tone rings out through the valley and if the villagers hear the tone they will be protected from all evil spirits. And if they are sick and hear the tone, they will be healed. We want you to have this replica because we know it represents you."

They gave me the story of the bell and had it inscribed "Good luck forever."

Isn't it just like Jesus? When Jesus speaks, it is like the tone of the bell ringing out. The authority His voice carries causes the enemy to flee. His voice is a bell of liberty. What an honor to represent Jesus.

I flew home in the peace of God. I began sharing with everyone how important it is to take Jesus with you.

We took Jesus to the streets of Austin. God was blessing people so fast. It was exciting! They started chasing us down, they wanted prayer so desperately. They were hungry for God. We got to declare that certain "sound"—just like the bell the monks rang in that far away place. And all who heard it were set free.

13

Gold Dust
September 5, 2010

My heart is confident in you, O God;
No wonder I can sing your praises with all
my heart! Wake up, lyre and harp!
I will wake the dawn with my song.
I will thank you, LORD, among all the
people. I will sing your praises among the
nations. For your unfailing love is higher
than the heavens. Your faithfulness
reaches to the clouds. Be exalted, O God,
above the highest heavens. May your
glory shine over all the earth.
—Psalm 108:1-5 NLT

My wife, Natalie, went to Redding, California to help three of our children settle into Bethel School of Ministry. She also wanted to attend a Bill Johnson conference. One of our daughters was moving from Phoenix to Redding. All these years I'd always come first. I wanted to honor her, so I sent her for a visit with our young adults. I could fend for myself at the house.

It was Sunday, September 5, 2010, early in the morning. I'm an early-morning guy. I'd just made coffee and was walking around the house when I told the Lord, "I sure miss Natalie."

The Lord spoke and told me, "I'm going to be closer to you." My thoughts were: *wow … wow!*

Then He said, "I want you to take these words." The words He gave me were: *Great and mighty is the Lord God Almighty, for He is worthy to be praised.*

He said, "I want you to take those words and I want you to repeat them over and over and over and over. Take your guitar and sing it over and over and over."

Great and mighty is the Lord God Almighty
For He's worthy to be praised.
Great and mighty is the Lord God Almighty
For He's worthy to be praised.
Great and mighty is the Lord God Almighty
For He's worthy to be praised.

God continued speaking to me: "These words don't talk about you or your problems, they talk about me. Dudley, I know how powerful it is."

He said, "When the people in the old times were moving after God, he said 'I will move.' They believed. But yet when they were marching to get the walls of Jericho down, God told them to bring the praise and worshipers out in front."

And here are all these people and that's what put me in awe. These people were all going to see the walls of Jericho come down and they *knew* that God was doing it for them. But God picked out the praise and worshipers to lead the way. In that day and age you'd think everybody would be worshiping God. I could understand the importance of it. It was like a battle.

> *But You are holy, O You Who dwell in the*
> *holy place where the praises of Israel,*
> *your people, [are offered].*
> —Psalm 22:3 AMP [author paraphrase]

I got my guitar, sat down, and started singing:

Great and mighty is the Lord God Almighty
For He's worthy to be praised.
Great and mighty is the Lord God Almighty
For He's worthy to be praised.
Great and mighty is the Lord God Almighty
For He's worthy to be praised.

The more I sang, the more and more intense I got. It was just me and our little dogs in the house. I have an electric guitar, so I cranked up the volume. I'm not a singer. I'm not a country western singer. I'm just Dudley. I usually sing in the shower when no one is around.

With the volume cranked up, I just sang out—giving it everything I had over and over:

Great and mighty is the Lord God Almighty
For He's worthy to be praised.
Great and mighty is the Lord God Almighty
For He's worthy to be praised.
Great and mighty is the Lord God Almighty
For He's worthy to be praised.

Suddenly, one of the dogs jumped off of the couch. I wondered what startled her, so I opened my eyes and took a look. I saw that when I was strumming my guitar, "glory gold dust" was flying off my arm. I was totally covered in it. The dog sensed what was going on in the room.

I kept pressing in and pressing in to experience more of Jesus and sang it over and over: *God is great and mighty is the Lord God Almighty for He's worthy to be praised.*

"Wow!" I said when I looked in the mirror, it's the "Glory of God." [God's glory is a physical manifestation of His transcendent reality. Exodus 33:18 NKJV notes]

I could feel God in the room with me. I could feel Him right there as I was just praising Him.

> And He said, "My Presence will go with you, and I will give you rest.
> —Exodus 33:14 NKJV

I'd hurt my back the previous night during a ministry time when I caught someone who was overcome by God's presence, slain in the spirit. I was in pain and that's one of the reasons I was really missing Natalie. When I had problems like that, she would massage my back.

I called my wife and asked her to pray for me. She prayed and suggested, "Go to church early and find somebody to pray for you as well."

I got cleaned up for church and washed all the gold dust off. Most of it was gone but a little bit of it was around my heart. Some was on me a little bit here and there. It wasn't as thick as when I was playing and singing. I went to the church looking for people to pray for me. I saw Cheryl and Joel. I knew they had attended a training program at the Austin Kingdom Academy School.

I also knew they were running after God. They were in the same class with my wife, Natalie. I said to myself, *these people know how to pray. I'll ask them.*

I wanted people who didn't beg for healing but would command healing in their prayers. When Cheryl and Joel prayed for me, I was totally healed.

They invited me over to their house that evening. I'd never been to their house so Cheryl texted the address to me and I put it in my GPS. I got in my car to head over and I started singing that song again. It was ringing in my head: *Great and mighty is the Lord God Almighty for He's worthy to be praised.*

I was lost in the spirit singing my new song: *Great and mighty is the Lord God Almighty for He's worthy to be praised.*

I was glad I had the GPS to get me there. I hoped I wouldn't get stopped by a policeman because I'm sure he would've given me a DUI. I was drunk all right—in the joy of the Lord.

Following the directions on the GPS, I showed up at the house. I was so wiped out from being in the Sprit I could hardly walk.

Joel looked at me in amazement. I was covered in the glory gold dust. There were large specs, as well as some very small fine dust particles. We just sat and talked about God.

We wondered together what the Gold Giver was doing with this visible sign of His Glory.

For the next few days, and then stretching into weeks, when God's gold dust came on me, there was a physical weight to it—the weight of His Glory.

God said to me, "The gold I put on you represents the gold in each and every person I will put before you. I want you to find my gold in them."

When you look through Jesus' eyes, you don't judge anymore. You find the gold in everybody. The love Jesus has for them is what matters."

I wondered if it would come back when I took a shower. I took a shower and washed it all off.

I asked Natalie to come and look—to see if it was all off. She came and looked at me when I came out of the shower. Natalie gave me a thorough inspection. It was all gone.

God once told me: "If you take the glory, you take the responsibility."

That was a humbling moment to prepare me for this. Since then my prayer has been: "God hide me in your glory, not that I be lifted up, but You O Lord, the Gold Maker, be lifted up."

I am the LORD, that is my name!
I will not give my glory to anyone else.
—Isaiah 42:8 NLT

I knew that God will not allow anyone to take His glory, but He will give it to you. He says He will not give His glory to another, but His Bride is not another.

The next morning we watched in amazement as the gold dust began to appear on my skin again, after I showered!

Seeing gold dust appear on people was not a new thing to us. We had seen it before during worship and when people were prayed for at Cathedral of Praise in Austin. But this was different.

Every time I washed it off, shaved it off, we could stand there and watch it come back. It would often increase during the day.

Each day it would look a little different— thicker in some areas, finer, or larger specks, even on my eyelashes. The more I enjoyed God or prayed for people, the more the increase came.

I could have tried to preserve it by not wash- ing it off, but then I would be wearing yesterday's glory. This taught us how to live in the fresh revelation of God's relationship every day. Every day with Him is so exciting.

Natalie and I know we are accountable that each day is an authentic return of God's glory gold dust.

> And the glory which You gave Me I have given them that they may be one just as We are one. [Jesus]
>
> —John 17:22 NKJV

Each day I stood in front of the mirror and watched it all come back again. All I would say is, "Great and mighty is the Lord God Almighty for He's worthy to be praised."

I could just have the thought: *Great and mighty is the Lord God Almighty for He's worthy to be praised.* And it would return.

The important thing was to give Him all the glory. I could feel the trembling of the marching feet of angels lining up, ready for action.

> Bless the LORD, you His angels, Who excel in strength, who do His word, Heeding the voice of His word.
> Bless the LORD, all you His hosts, You ministers of His who do His pleasure.
>
> —Psalm 103:20-21 NKJV

The next day happened to be a holiday, Labor Day. I went to town shopping for a large toolbox.

I entered a pawn shop. An old man came over and said, "You have gold dust all over you."

I looked at him and smiled and said, "Yeah, when I'm in the presence of God this comes on me."

"Will you pray for me?" he asked.

I prayed for him and tears were running down his face. I realized: *I am an instrument of God.*

A tangible sign showed this stranger the presence of God, and he knew God was listening, and that He cared. Seeing the "glory gold dust" on me, built up his faith in God—God could answer prayer.

"What's on me is what's inside of you," I told him. That seemed to speak to him.

I was consumed with the need to pray for people. I didn't force anything on anyone. People were drawn to me and wanted a touch from God.

On my way to a department store to look for the toolbox, I stopped at a gas station to get a candy bar. When I put it on the counter, the gold dust was falling all over. While I was trying to wipe it up, the clerk said, "You're shiny and sparkling."

"When I get in the presence of God this happens," I said.

I told him what had happened at the pawn shop. He asked if I would pray for him. There were people in line to buy stuff, but I just took his hand and prayed for him. I thought, *WOW*. They're just coming out of the bushes. This guy has other things to do but he wants prayer.

I bought a very large heavy toolbox at the department store and took it home. Unloading it by myself would definitely put my lower back to the test.

I thought, *my friends prayed for me and I know my back is healed.* So I lifted it out of the back of my truck. That proved it! Praise God! I was pain free!

One of the drawers didn't have a key for the lock so I had to go back to the store. I told the clerk I didn't want to bring the heavy toolbox all the way back inside. I just wanted him to give me a new key for the lock and I'd put it on myself. He said I'd have to talk to the manager. Then he brought the manager down.

As the manager walked up, she said, "You have gold dust all over you." She knew exactly what it was and asked for prayer.

So there I was praying for the department manager. Meanwhile, lots of people came for prayer.

When I got back in the car, I sang: *Great and mighty is the Lord God Almighty for He's worthy to be praised.* I would sing it to Him over and over again. It was my joy to praise Him.

The first week as the glory gold dust came on me, it was like carrying heavy weights. I felt like I'd had an intense workout. I was worn out. The Lord told me He would strengthen my legs so I could carry His glory.

Many times when I washed it off, and Natalie inspected me, a fear came over me: *What would people think if the gold isn't there anymore? They will think I've been up to no good or done something wrong.*

The Lord said, "Dudley, you wear it well."

It was such a humbling moment to hear my King say that to me. When the Lord told me that, I put it all to rest.

It really doesn't matter what others think. I'm just glad He trusted me with such an amazing thing. There are a lot of things in the world I would not want to have put on me. I could have been covered in mud! To God be all the glory!

Some people have a problem with it. Well, my wife and I had a big problem with it too! I felt it should be on my wife, not me. My Natalie knows the Bible and has memorized much of it. I think she's more deserving than me. But our God is a grace God. Because of Jesus, we all qualify.

For it is God who commanded light to shine out of darkness, who has shone in our hearts to give the light of the knowledge of the glory of God in the face of Jesus Christ.
—2 Corinthians 4:6 NKJV

God said, "You wash it off every day. The glory I put on you today is not the glory I need on you for tomorrow."

We go from glory to glory because God doesn't want a relationship from the past, he wants a daily relationship. He wants you to be a light to get His glory out there.

But we all with unveiled face, beholding as in a mirror the glory of the Lord, are being transformed into the same image from glory to glory, just as by the Spirit of the Lord.
—2 Corinthians 3:18 NKJV

I was part of a wedding party so I went to Oklahoma for the wedding. Driving I was singing the song: *Great and mighty is the Lord God Almighty for He's worthy to be praised.*

Finally all the coffee I drank caught up with me. I pulled into the Ada, Oklahoma rest stop. On my way to the restroom, I saw a truck driver. He was limping pretty badly and our paths were going to intersect.

I'm compelled by God's glory on me. I don't even have a choice anymore about praying for people. Now I have a different mindset. I'm bound by His Love.

I asked the guy if I could pray for him.

He looked at me and said, "You're glittery, dude."

"When I get in the presence of God, this gold dust comes on me. Can I pray for you?" I said.

"Sure, buddy," he said.

I started to lean over and the Lord directed me get on my knees. We were pretty close to the restroom and I'm holding his knee. This is

138

not a church and this guy doesn't know how to act. He started screaming with joy. I could feel God's healing touch going out of me, out of my arm into him, and the healing taking place.

An older lady walked up at the same time and she stopped in her tracks.

There was also a young couple sitting at the map area and this guy is screaming like I'm killing him as God's glory is filling him.

I looked up and he looked up. He says, "It's like brand-new!" He is moving his leg and jumping up and down.

Then the older lady said, "I want that golden guy to pray for me!"

I told the truck driver, "You can only keep what you give away."

She was a really cute little lady, so I went over to her to pray for her. The truck driver is like Superman. He is behind her in a flash with his hands on her shoulder to pray for her. He got the message.

I put my hand on her other shoulder and she says, "Honey, it's not my shoulder that hurts, it's my tummy." She took my hand and put it on her stomach!

I thought: *This is not the proper way a man is supposed to minister to a woman.*

I feel sorry for women in Jesus' time because men were not allowed to lay hands on a woman in that culture.

We just prayed for her and she said, "Oh... That just feels so good. My tummy feels so good!"

I told her, "You only get to keep what you give away."

Then the young couple sitting there stood up. The woman asks, "What is this gold dust all about?"

"What's going on," I said, "is when I get in God's glory, He puts this gold dust on me. When I pray for people, it increases. I've been praying for a lot of people. Can I pray for you?"

He said, "Wait ... wait, I don't know."

I knew what he was talking about. He was just like me years ago. I wanted more of God but I didn't want it to change or interfere with my lifestyle.

His wife was pregnant, very pregnant, and not just like a couple months pregnant but close to full term.

"Yeah, we want some prayer. We want that," she said.

"God's not trying to change you. God just wants you get to know Him. God's love will compel you to change. Everything with God is by choice. He loves you and He wants to give you all He can give," I said to the guy.

"We want that." She was speaking up for both of them.

Immediately, the truck driver and the old lady jumped behind them to pray. They knew they only get to keep what they give away! I held their hands and we prayed.

After I prayed, I turned to both of them and said, "God loves you and God is going to move fast on your behalf. Now that you have received Jesus Christ as your Lord and Savior, God likes to show off that He is God."

"You all be blessed!" I said. Then I went to the bathroom and left the rest area.

I'm driving down the Interstate and was only about seven minutes from the rest stop when a car came zooming up. They were honking at me. I thought, *OK. Oklahoma crazies.*

I look over and it is the young couple from the rest stop. She is waving and waving for me to pull over. I pulled over—way off the Interstate. I don't like stopping on the highway.

As soon as I put it in park, she jumps out of her car and came running back to me. She said, "Look I've got to tell you something. I'm so glad we caught up to you!"

"What's up?" I asked.

"You told us God would move fast, on our behalf. As soon as you left, that little old lady came up to us. She said the Lord told her to give us $1000. She wrote a check right then and there and gave it to us."

Then she showed me the check. They said, "We never told you, but we need deposit money for an apartment before the baby is born."

Because they had a dog, they needed exactly $1000 for the deposit and didn't know how they would get it. She was so excited she was jumping up and down, amazed at how fast God moved. The young man was also jumping up and down. It was a crazy scene!

Then a state trooper pulled up behind us. I thought: *I look like I'm coming from a party with all God's gold dust on me.*

I was leaning up against my truck. I was so lost in the Spirit.

This may be the beginning of a prison ministry! I thought.

"Is there a problem here?" the trooper asked.

"Everything's okay, Officer. Be blessed," I said. So he left.

I said good-bye to the couple, pulled back on the Interstate, and went on to the wedding.

14

Oklahoma Hotel Celebration
September 19, 2010

And it is impossible to please God without faith. Anyone who wants to come to him must believe that God exists and that he rewards those who sincerely seek him.
—Hebrews 11:6 NLT

I arrived at the motel in Oklahoma wh3ere most of the wedding party was staying. It had off-site parking so I had to park some distance from the motel.

Early the next morning, God woke me up. I dressed and went to the office downstairs. The valet parking is open twenty-four hours a day so there were people there that early.

The valet attendant said to me, "You're all a glitter."

I told him when I get in the presence of God this comes on me. I told him I'd been praying for people.

"Can you pray for me?" he asked. He told me he wanted to know God more. He really poured his heart out. I prayed, sat with him, and encouraged him.

"You only get to keep what you give away," I said.

He told me he got off work at 7 a.m. so I left.

I went to the wedding trying to hide so I wouldn't upstage the bride. Not easy with the "gold dust manifestation." My goal was not to become a spectacle and create a problem for the bride on her wedding day. This was her big day.

This was kind of hard when I'm sitting there like a disco ball and there's a light shining on me. I did my best to honor them. I got to pray for a lot of people.

That evening after the wedding, I headed back to the hotel and parked upstairs in the convention center garage. When I went down, I had to go through this long dark eerie hallway. When I opened up the doors, I was about 100 yards from the front of the hotel.

I heard somebody yelling loudly, "Dudley!" He kept shouting, "Dudley, Dudley!"

I wondered, *what in the world is going on here.* It was the parking attendant from that morning. He ran full blast over to me.

Some of the people from the wedding party were with me and they were wondering what this was all about.

Again he said, "Dudley …Dudley. I've got a lot to tell you."

I would guess he was a man in his early thirties. He said, "I went home and told my mama about the golden guy. I told my mama what the golden guy was saying. So mom called her two sisters, my aunts, and they came over to our house.

"All the cousins came over and they're all sitting there this morning. All morning I was telling them all what you said that God was doing and about finding the gold in everybody."

When he got close to the end of what he was saying, his aunt said, "Okay, everybody, let's grab our hands together. We want to make sure Jesus is our Lord and Savior."

"Dudley, I had eight cousins come to Jesus!" he said.

"That's really awesome!" I said.

By this time, people were gathering around us listening. There were even three or four homeless guys standing there. People in the restaurant were also hearing it.

The restaurant was closing down for the evening, so the staff brought their chairs out in front of the restaurant where we could continue talking. The night clerks propped open the door so they could still hear the phone ring in the motel and listen to me.

There were maybe seventeen in the group sitting there. I preached and taught for hours. I told them what's in me is in you. At 3:15 a.m. I had them line up and prayed for them,

"I give to you, now you need to give to others," I said. "We are one body and if I just give out and give out, I become like a deflated balloon. If all you do is receive, you get like a balloon blown up and ready to explode. But if we go back and forth giving and receiving, then we have life. There are people behind you waiting for you to give the word out to them. I prayed for you, now you have a special word for each other and me."

When we were doing this, it was like having a church service. I told them to put their left hand on the person next to them and ask God for a word for the person to the left.

Everyone had a word for the person to their left. Every word was some type of encouragement. Even the homeless guys had an encouraging word. Then we did it for the person on the right.

Then I had them give a word to me and every word was consistent. Over and over, I heard the love of God. Here is a group of people who weren't in church, not church-goers, but now they're in the Spirit and moving in the spiritual gifts.

"We've been running after God all night," I said. "Now let's do something religious. Let's take a tithe offering."

They just busted out laughing because that's the only thing about church that they could associate with.

"We've just had church. You are equipped and empowered. Now you can go out and do what you were doing tonight," I said.

As we broke up, there was a dressed-up lady hugging the homeless. Then the homeless were hugging the others. We all saw people as God sees them. We were all the same. We were all one family. I saw the love of God they had for each other and it was expressed with care and compassion. Some of the people were giving food from the restaurant and money to the homeless.

I needed to get some rest, so I told them I had to go back to my room. They asked me to come back tomorrow.

As I walked away, I said, "Tag you're it! You only get to keep what you give away."

I was just on fire. Did it cost me time? Yes. Did it cost me anything really? No.

Why?

Because Jesus paid it all.

I died back on September 16, 1997 in that motel room. I died and now Jesus lives in me!

I've got to get out of here and drive back to Austin. I need to get there before Natalie arrives home.

15

Unusual Encounters
September 23, 2010

*But sanctify the Lord God in your hearts,
and always be ready to give a defense
to everyone who asks you a reason for
the hope that is in you, with meekness
and fear.*

—1 Peter 3:15 NKJV

I have had so many incidents around Texas where people just come up to me and comment on the gold. This usually turns into a ministry opportunity.

A fun event happened when I was walking into the supermarket. I only needed a few items. A Hispanic guy was looking at me and following me around. Everywhere I went, there he was. It seemed strange because he was not picking anything up to purchase.

I thought, *hmmm, that's strange. I guess I'm just drawing attention.*

I finally went to check out with my five items and this guy is standing beside me and doesn't have anything to purchase. This was weird. I made my purchase and went out into the parking lot.

He followed me into the parking lot calling out, "Pardon, Pardon!"

He told me he was a pastor from Chihuahua, a city in Mexico, and was here visiting his sister. He told me he had "kidney rocks" but he meant kidney stones.

He said the Lord told him to go to this supermarket and find the golden guy. So when he saw me he knew I was the golden guy. He said God told him to tell me the number eighteen and I would know what that meant.

I knew what this meant—it was the eighteenth day that I'd had the gold dust on me.

"Will you pray for me?" he asked.

I laid my hands on his back. Once again, it was like a bazooka! God hit him and it blasted the dude. It was just the love of God that was poured out and he was healed, no pain!

I'm just a simple guy but these "God things" are happening outside the walls of the church. It was a supermarket.

I get blessed because I get to pray for people. I realize their concerns are more than my concerns, they are also God's concerns.

In September 2010, I went to a conference at a Houston church. My wife and I got a hotel room. We had signed up for the conference months before this manifestation had ever come on me. We were going down there just to listen, to see people hungry for God, to see Georgian Banov and other leaders.

Everybody Christian has a word from God. As I grow in God, I've learned from this process: We've got to stop judging people.

God told me to look at everyone as if they are learning. We don't necessarily agree with everybody, but if we look at them as growing in God—we can love them even if we don't agree with them.

When we got to our motel, the staff really opened their eyes when they saw the gold on me. My wife and I were going the next morning to have breakfast and it was just more opportunities.

We were sitting there eating and a man was sitting in a nearby chair. God told me to go pray for his heart, specifically for his heart. I got up immediately.

I told him, "I'm attending this glory confer- ence and we believe in healing. The Lord spoke to me and told me to come over and ask you if I could pray for your heart."

His adult daughter was sitting next to him. She turned to me and said, "I'm a lawyer, what did you say?"

I thought, *whoa, am I going to get sued on this deal?*

"God told me to come over and pray for his heart," I said.

"Who told you?" she asked.

"God told me," I responded.

"He just had open heart surgery and is in severe pain, and the pain hasn't left," she said.

So I asked him again, "May I pray for your heart?"

He shook his head "yes."

I prayed for him.

Immediately, his pain went away.

When I walked away, I asked the Lord what that was all about.

The Lord said, "It is quite simple. She repre- sents the law but I am mercy and grace. Jesus will heal them all with his mercy and grace."

When we went to the conference, people would see the gold dust on me and they would have to make a choice. I could see really quickly that they either chose to believe or not believe. If they didn't believe, I blessed them.

What I observed was that when people saw the gold, their faith would rise. As I prayed for them, it was miracle after miracle after miracle.

I would get there early and start praying for people. I prayed for people throughout the entire conference. Morning, afternoon, and all through the evening I ministered. It was hard to leave. I just couldn't say no. I was compelled to keep praying.

One large lady walked up to me, looked me in the eye, and said, "I'm deformed. I was born missing two bones in my inner ear, so I am deaf in this ear. In the other ear, I can hear perfectly."

I knew God was smiling and I could sense His excitement. I could see the line drawn in the sand. *God, you can do this miracle!*

With God, this is a slam dunk! I was excited because I saw God smile.

"In the name of Jesus," I said. Almost before I finished saying the name of Jesus, I heard this pop.

She got a very serious look on her face as if she's looking right through me.

Then I realized, *She's not looking at me at all, she is looking at Jesus. Jesus has just healed her ear.*

"I can hear, I can hear out of that ear!" she said, as the tears started flowing.

It was the same way with arms, elbows, eyes, necks, legs, and backs. As I prayed for people, others would see the healings and they would line up to be prayed for. The ministry just went on. People are so hungry to see God move, and receive His healing and blessing.

The more I ministered the more the gold dust came on me. At one point, the side of my face was so covered that I almost looked like the phantom of the opera.

People would ask me, "Why are you a special guy?"

"I am not a special guy," I said.

One lady asked for prayer and said that she wanted the gold dust to come on her. We prayed for her. I got an e-mail later that she's having sapphire dust coming on her stomach area.

Around midnight we were driving home from Houston after the conference, when one of the pastors called. Someone had left a voicemail at their home that gold dust was forming on the face of someone in their congregation.

We were running after God.

During the whole conference, I was pre-occupied with how we can get people to pray for others. I would pray for one and then tell them: "You only get to keep what you give away." So then I'd have that person pray for the next one in line.

God has lined us up for these days we're in. I see all kinds of miracles from people passing it on.

I had a pastor call me when we got back home. He said, "I've been a pastor for thirty some years. I am calling to ask forgiveness for my judgment of you. I watched you at the conference. I hung around the back to be unnoticed and watched you. I watched the gold come out on your face and I had a problem with that. I could see it increase on you and I really had a problem with that—for about a week. I took it to the Lord and the Lord said: 'You don't believe. You don't believe Me or my Word.'"

I told him God loves Him, and be blessed.

Sometimes we put God in a box and don't realize that God can do what He wants.

But our God is in heaven; he does what he pleases.

—Psalm 115:3 NKJV

I went to pick up items I needed for a trip I was about to take. I went to the supermarket, grabbed a handbasket, and headed down the aisle.

There was woman in front of me looking at a shelf and a man behind me waiting. As I waited for her to make her decision, she looked up at me and said, "OK, I need to know what the glitter is all about!"

I told her that when I get into the presence of God this comes on me.

The guy behind me leans over and says, "It's a proven fact that the human mind cannot handle death. The mind makes up a deity because the mind can't handle the fact that the body dies or goes into the ground and rots. This is a proven fact!"

I turned and was looking right at him. Immediately, the Lord gave me a word of knowledge for him.

I said, "Look, seven years ago at the mountain of the gods, you were in a skiing accident. You broke your wrist. The broken bone severed the nerve in your hand so you've had no feeling in your hand since then. It healed wrong so you don't have flexibility in moving your wrist. I'm going to pray for you and God is going to heal that hand and restore the nerves so you can feel the love of God!"

There was no visible sign that he had any problems with his wrist. I grabbed his wrist and said, "In the name of Jesus, you are healed."

He lifted his hand up, flexed his hand and a stunned look spread over his face.

"It works, it works, it works! He's real, He's real, He's real!" Tears began to profusely flow. He just started hugging me and crying so much, my shirt was getting wet.

"You nailed it," he said. "Everything you said was true! How can God forgive me because I've been telling everybody this?" he said.

"God already has," I said.

We put our baskets down, I put my arm around him, and we began to walk out of the store.

The lady raised her hand and said really loudly, "Praise God, Praise the Lord!"

You could hear everyone in that area saying, "Praise the Lord!"

I led him outside so he could sit in his car. I stood by the driver's door talking to him about the Lord.

I told him, "Let's make sure that Jesus is your Savior." I led him in a salvation prayer.

"You only get to keep what you give away," I said.

He replied, "I'm going to work and tell everybody!"

A few weeks later, I was again at the supermarket. As I was leaving the store and heading out to the parking lot, there was a young couple that had paint on their face. They were pretty wild and you could tell they were loaded.

When they saw me they said, "You really know how to party!" They asked me for five dollars.

I pointed toward them and said, "Jesus is going to take you higher than you've ever been. God's going to make your body reject the drugs. You're not even going to like them anymore."

Immediately, they both bent over and started vomiting. It was ballistic, right there in the parking lot!

I heard the Lord say, "I have them." So I knew it was in His hands, and I walked away.

I attended a conference at a church in Austin. Bill Johnson, senior pastor of Bethel Church in Redding, California, was the speaker. I could feel God really moving in that place. We saw many people being healed. As I was leaving, many people saw the gold dust and wanted prayer.

I prayed for a lady that had hearing problems. I laid my hands on her ears and prayed. I asked if there was any change on a scale from 1 to 10. She said it was like a one point change.

I got so excited. Any improvement is a sign something is happening. I knew she would be healed.

I kept praying and praying. I stuck with it, even though my body said it's enough.

"Don't let it go," the Lord said. So I just kept praying.

She was totally healed.

People will run to where God is moving. They are hungry.

16

God's Presence In Asia
October 2010

*Be strong and very courageous. Be careful
to obey all the instructions Moses gave
you. Do not deviate from them, turning
either to the right or to the left. Then you
will be successful in everything you do.
This is my command—be strong and
courageous! Do not be afraid or
discouraged. For the Lord your God is
with you wherever you go.*
—Joshua 1:7, 9 NLT

Some months earlier, I sold technology to a country in Asia. They made 3-D models and wanted me to come, review their changes, and give them ideas. It was to be a quick trip.

I needed a new passport and to get my visa for multiple entries into the country.

The passport picture was a challenge. They couldn't get a clear picture without God's glory dust showing up. It was on me pretty heavy.

"What's the story with this glitter?" the photographer asked me.

So I told her this happens when I get in the presence of God. She asked me to pray with her. She got very serious and I prayed for her and her son.

"I don't normally do this," she told me and gave me a big hug. When I went back to pick up my pictures, she was excited to see me. Then the other lady that worked there asked for prayer.

I told her, "God isn't trying to change you, but the love of God will cause you to change." It really touched me how much God loved her.

Natalie and one of her friends drove me to the Houston airport. I was four hours early for my flight because of commitments Nat's friend had back in Austin.

I was curious what was going to happen when I went through security and the metal detectors. I'm all glittery and shining for God. The TSA agents were looking at me pretty seriously. As I went through the metal detector, they asked what the gold was, and so I told them.

Then one of them swabbed it, trying to get a sample, but it didn't come off very well. They did test it to see if it was explosive. While I was putting my shoes back on, two of the TSA guys asked for prayer. We held hands and I prayed God's blessing on them both.

As I walked around looking in the shops at the airport, one of the gals working at a watch shop asked, "Where have you been? What party have you been to?"

"I've been at God's party. When I get in God's presence this comes on me," I told her.

As soon as she heard that, she teared up. I had walked by her shop earlier, and she'd pointed at me and laughed. Now she was under conviction.

"It's all right. God's having a blast with all this."

Most people are looking for God's gifts and that is so narrow. Our God is boundless and in Him we have no need.

When I got on the plane, the flight attendant took notice of me. Finally, at the end of the flight, she asked me about the gold dust and so I told her.

Then she said, "I don't ever do this, but could you pray for my mother?"

I could feel God's hope flow into her as we prayed. I was the last one off the plane. As I got to the front, the other stewardess asked for prayer. So I prayed with her. The pilot just watched it all with a big grin on his face.

At JFK airport, I had a four-hour lay-over. I had to go through security again. When the woman took my passport, she looked at me and then did a double-take. I could tell she wanted something, so I just took her hand and blessed her. Going through security again, no buzzers went off, but they still took me aside and gave me the once over with the wand. Their eyes never left my face. It was funny.

At the gate, I started talking to a man and his son. The father wanted to hear, but the son, a young man in his thirties, looked like he just wanted to run. Then he made some kind of sarcastic comment and walked off. I didn't hear it but his father was embarrassed and started apologizing for his son.

"Don't worry about it," I told him, "He's under God's protection through your covenant."

He asked more about me and about God.

"Are you a pastor?" he asked.

"No, Bud, I'm just a regular guy from an oil patch running after God."

Then a young woman who worked as a massage therapist and was waiting to open for business came over. She started asking me questions. She was really excited.

"God is always moving," I told her. "If we ask Him specifically, He will reveal the mysteries so we can bless our world."

She was concerned for her brother, so I asked God to reveal Himself to her, and that her covenant would protect her brother.

> *Believe on the Lord Jesus Christ and you will be saved, you and your household."*
> —Acts 16:31 NKJV

I boarded the plane and found my seat in economy. I sat there sparkling with gold dust. A couple came up and said, "We see the glory of God all over you. Can you come back and talk with us?"

I went to the back of the plane, where drinks were set out for the passengers. I met the other members of their group that were traveling together. They loved Jesus and were going to the nations to preach the gospel. It was a good feeling to know I wasn't the only one God was sending. I prayed for all of them.

> *Go into all the world and preach the gospel to every creature.*
> —Mark 16:15 NKJV

While on the airplane, the glory dust was on my hands and face real strong. When I got off the plane, I went through temperature scanners which allow them to see if you have a fever. I was curious if I would read normal and I did.

†

The immigration officer spent more time with me than on my earlier trip to Asia. He kept looking at me and typing and looking at me and typing some more. After I cleared customs, I went into the restroom to check myself out. No gold dust was visible. It had disappeared. When I checked my chest, the glory dust was heavy on my chest around my heart.

I had another long lay-over in the gateway city of the country. I was sitting there with my bags when God said, "Look at those two guys."

I glanced over and saw two average Asian men. Nothing out of the ordinary.

I had a chance to pray for an Australian couple. He was an airline pilot and they asked for prayer for their son. They said he was a wild one.

I told them, "We're all a little wild."

His wife held my hand the entire time. I had this great prayer opportunity and the gold dust wasn't even showing!

As I went to the gate for my next flight, those two men God had pointed out to me were there. I thought *they must be on my flight.*

Upon arrival, my hosts picked me up in a private car and took me to spend the night in a hotel and get a fresh start in the morning.

While I was checking in, I looked over my shoulder. There stood those same two men from the airport. Now I began to wonder, *how did they get here as fast as we got here? What's going on?*

That night in my hotel room, I had a good time of praise and worship with the Lord.

The next morning, just like I did on my first trip to Asia, I presented the people of this country to Him. The interpreter picked me up and the glory dust would sort of blink on for a minute. Then it would disappear when I was around people, but it always seemed to remain on my heart.

The interpreter saw it, but still didn't believe it. I told him that this comes on me when I'm in God's presence.

Then God said, "Show him your chest." I unbuttoned my shirt and showed him the gold dust heavy around my heart.

Then I said, "If you have a building you need an architect, right? We have man, so who is the architect?"

He didn't know quite how to respond.

God's favor was everywhere. A limo picked me up. We arrived at the manufacturing plant. I got the royal treatment again. I did reviews and teachings during the day. They had a meeting scheduled with officials of the oil company and because of the favor of God, I was included.

When I got back to my new hotel, there were my two buddies from the airport again.

I was definitely being followed. This was a whole new set of circumstances.

The next business meeting I had with this company the Lord told me, "They are going to test you."

Every question they asked went through the interpreter. That was good for me because while they asked me the question in their language, God was already giving me the answers before I heard it in English. He told me exactly what to say. So I knew the answer before I knew what the question was going to be.

Some of the material they asked me about, I had no knowledge of, but God gave me the answer. He gave me even deeper knowledge in areas I was familiar with. After about ten

168

minutes, the questioning stopped and they asked me, "How did you get all this knowledge?"

My answer was, "God is good." That's just truth. Praise God.

✝

My hosts decided to take me to see a temple. It was a huge temple and filled with monks and incense. While the interpreter was in the restroom, I said, "Come on Jesus."

So I went right up to the big golden Buddha and said, "Buddha, this is Jesus. Jesus, this is Buddha. Buddha, you may be covered in gold, but I'm covered in the glory of God, the true gold. Jesus is alive and you've died."

The interpreter came back and took me away from there, but I sensed Jesus' pleasure.

The interpreter took me to the city to get a part to fix a computer problem. We were walking along when suddenly we found ourselves in the midst of a huge anti-government protest march. Thousands of angry people carrying banners stopped traffic and shouted anti-government slogans. I waited on the steps leading to the strip mall while he went in to get the part.

I looked at these thousands of people milling around on bikes and motorcycles. My heart just went out to them.

Then I could feel Jesus standing right beside me. I leaned against Him.

"Look how many are going to bow before me," He said.

Sooner or later, we're all going to bow before Jesus, but I was looking at a multitude of those who would be in the "later" category.

> *For it is written* (Isa. 45:23): *"As I live, says the Lord, Every knee shall bow to Me, and every tongue shall confess to God."*
> —Romans 14:11 NKJV

People began to come up the steps right beside me. Lines of people walking single file came right past me.

This must be happening because I'm a foreigner.

But God said, "Watch this."

As if He'd snapped His fingers, the crowds started to walk up the eighty-foot wide steps in a normal way.

Then I noticed alleys and streets full of these green hats converging on the square like army ants streaming towards their mound. There were so many, I'd never seen anything like it. I started to get my camera out to take a picture of the banners and all, but the Lord said, "No, Dudley."

Next thing I knew, the interpreter grabbed my arm saying, "We don't need to be here." He quickly led me down the stairs to the basement and through alleyways and insane traffic. We crossed this huge busy street. There are no organized crosswalks, no traffic light, they make three lanes out of two. It's crazy.

I was right behind him. Then I lost track of him. I saw this car coming at a high speed right for me. I had no fear as I thought, *this is it.* I had a feeling this was a one way trip—this is it!

The car screeched to a stop with its bumper touching my pants leg. The interpreter jumped back to get me and really told this guy off. I just stood there thanking God. He'd spared my life again.

God's favor kept opening more and more opportunities. They flew me back to the large gateway city. Then the company driver and interpreter took me to another airport. It had connections to the city I needed to go to for the next round of meetings with top government and company officials.

My two buddies were already there, still following me. I started talking with a pilot from South Africa. He was very unhappy with the crowded airport and long delays and told me, "God's punishing us."

"God doesn't work that way. He's a loving God." I said. "We do have an adversary. He can't hurt you, but he can steal your joy. God protects us but the devil, if he can take the song out of your heart, he's got you."

He asked if I was a preacher. I told him, "No. Not at all. I'm in the oil business. There are no preachers in the oil fields." We had a good laugh over that.

Then I told him, "You're a pilot and I'm a pilot. When we're flying high you can hear God. Listen to Him."

He wanted to be hired by a particular airline, so I prayed with him in agreement.

"If that's your desire, God probably put that desire on your heart so you can carry His people." I told him.

We sat pretty close together on the airplane so we kept talking.

"God moves in mysterious ways," I said.

"How's that," he asked.

"Well, sometimes He can put things on you, you don't understand."

"Like what?"

"Like this," I said and I opened my shirt.

172

"Wow! What is that?"

I showed him the glory dust around my heart.

"Why don't you collect it?" he asked.

"It disappears. I shower it all off every day and shave. It comes back when I spend time with God."

"Why?" He asked.

"You know what it does? It makes you ask the question. I don't know why but I can tell you one thing it does. It makes you make a decision. Either you believe it or you don't. You believe it, you're blessed. Don't believe, you're still blessed. Do you think this is an accident that we met? Maybe God arranged this whole trip just for you and this very moment."

Then he wanted to confess his failings from the past.

"God loves you, brother, and He forgives you. Don't focus on what you've done. Focus on what you're going to do."

He was quiet the rest of the trip, in his own place with the Lord.

When we landed, I helped a lady who was overwhelmed by the entire process of getting her bags and making her connections home. She'd never traveled by herself before and felt alone and frightened. When I got her all taken care of, she said, "You've been such a blessing. I don't know how I'll manage without you."

"God promises us in His Word that He'll take us by the hand and lead us. You are not alone. He is with you," I said. We prayed for safe travels for her and His peace and she said she felt His love.

> *If I take the wings of the morning or*
> *dwell in the uttermost parts of the sea,*
> *Even there shall Your hand lead me,*
> *and Your right hand shall hold me.*
> —Psalm 139:9-10 AMP

There was this mad dash from the airport to my hotel because the top officials were already there and waiting to start the meeting.

Of course, I'd been delayed in baggage taking care of that lady. But God knows.

Again, I was met by the favor of God.

I presented the product and explained more about it and the deal we were cutting. They agreed to go ahead with the deal and a high official declared, "It's a done deal."

They presented me with another award which gave me freedom to come and go and travel anywhere in their country whenever I wanted to. No visas required. They rearranged their schedule so we could finish all our business.

I could return to the USA in time to see my son before he deployed to Afghanistan.

They all escorted me to my room and arranged for a car and interpreter to pick me up the next morning and give me a tour of the city.

I would usually get up a couple hours early and be alone worshipping God. I'd sing the song God gave me over and over again in my heart. Just being with Him in the security of my room, I'd be covered in the glory gold dust. Then I'd walk from my room to the elevator. I checked my reflection in the mirror in the elevator and the gold dust was gone. It had all disappeared except for what was on my heart.

I went to check out of my hotel and wait for the assigned interpreter. There were my two buddies again. *How did they know what time I'd be coming down? Wild.*

I met Betty, my interpreter for this city, and we waited outside about forty minutes for the driver. Driving to our first destination, Betty told me about the different points of interest.

First, we went to a busy tourist area. There were metal detectors and a strong security presence there. It was so crowded I found it hard to even walk. It was crammed with people and I asked God to bless them all.

Next we went to a temple area. Betty explained everything to me. This big square represents the earth and the center represents the heavens.

"I can handle that. I'm going to heaven. Do you want to go to heaven? Let's pray," I said.

As we came into the heaven section, there was a large dome-shaped rock. Twice a year at summer and winter solstice, a high official goes and offers prayers for the good of the people. They believe it is a portal and the heavens open.

So I'm looking around and thinking, *Thank God, we are His portal, and we can touch people and pray. We don't have to find a special place.*

I went over and stretched out my arm over that rock declaring, "We are God's portal." All of a sudden, it began raining gold dust. Like a fountain pouring from my arm, I was being consumed by it. I forgot where I was. But it disappeared before it reached the rock.

If I could see the gold dust, others could see it too. Immediately, about 250 people pressed in to have a look.

Then I heard these "Ahh's" of amazement and Asian language being spoken all over.

They started charging in, grabbing at the gold dust, and trying to touch me. It was frenzy, out of control. I managed to pull my arm in, and it stopped. I'm taller than most of them. I could see the security force coming in from all sides. You just don't start a disturbance in this place.

The interpreter quickly pulled me through the people. We were running, lost in the crowd. We ran into a tunnel to cross the street. I saw my two buddies there. They had been following me all day. The crowd is running and the crowd is gaining on us as we approach the line waiting to pass through the next metal detector. The line parted and we were waved through the metal detectors. Then they closed it down. We didn't see my two buddies again the rest of the trip.

The interpreter found a place for us to eat that had more American-type food. We started talking about what she'd seen that day.

I told her, "God loves all these people and He's coming for them. God isn't trying to overthrow your government, He just loves you. You can talk to Him whenever you want. You don't need me. Ask God and He'll show how good He is. Ask Him to talk to you. He will. He loves you."

We talked more and we prayed. I told her the next time I come, she would meet my wife and she would show her more than I could.

At the airport, I gave her some gifts that they'd given me. She really appreciated it. We exchanged emails and it was all good.

I got through departure with a couple of strange looks but no problems. I prayed for a lot of people. When I got on the plane, I was getting funny looks.

"What's with all the glitter on you?" a lady asks.

It was back.

During my layover in Atlanta, I got to pray with a couple of police officers.

Natalie picked me up at the port city of Wilmington, North Carolina airport. We met our son, Kenny, at his home and he drove us to a restaurant for dinner. Natalie had a recording of the song I got from the Lord on a CD. As it begins to play in the car, Kenny bobs his head along with the music.

After dinner, we went walking on the nearby beach. Natalie was having a hard time with Kenny's deployment. I asked God to comfort her.

She found a whole seashell. No cracks, nothing missing or broken. God said to her spirit, "This is Kenny. I'm keeping him."

One thing God showed me in Asia is that we must go 100 percent. He's not a part-way God. There's not a 50/50 chance. He's not a gambler. We have to give it all and He'll give it all to us. There's no equation for God. We just need to be 100 percent. He's not a fraction God. He's a whole God. He loves us. He wants to break through to us. He needs us to align up with Him then He can release the riches of heaven.

> *You shall love the LORD your God with*
> *all your heart, and with all your soul,*
> *and with all your strength.*
> —Deuteronomy 6:5 NKJV

If you think you're the source of income for your family or business, you're going to have setbacks. But trade jobs with God, let Him be the provider, and He'll bless above and beyond.

I want to give everything God has given me to everybody. When we love and feel responsible for others, we lift them up, we stop judging.

God's not trying to take away from us. He wants to give us all things.

> *He who did not withhold or spare [even] His own Son but gave Him up for us all, will He not also with Him freely and graciously give us all [other] things.*
> —Romans 8:32 AMP

So whatever you do, don't hold anything back, give it all for God.

No matter how distant we find ourselves from God, He loves us and nothing can separate us from His love.

> *For I am persuaded that neither death nor life, nor angels nor principalities nor powers, nor things present nor things to come, nor height nor depth nor any other created thing, shall be able to separate us from the love of God which is in Christ Jesus our Lord.*
> —Romans 8:38-39 NKJV

17

God Is Still Working
February 2, 2011

No eye has seen, no ear has heard, and no mind has imagined what God has prepared for those who love him.
—1 Corinthians 2:9 NLT

For all of you who may be wondering about my spiritual growth, no I have not attended a Bible School. After my motel experience and seeing the spiritual warfare, which is all around us, I knew I wanted to grow in Him and learn more about God.

I knew I needed to read His biography, which is the Bible. Trust me—it was not a cake walk. My flesh did not want to read, but the hunger in my spirit kept me reading.

Like anything in life, the initial start into what improves you, tends to rub you raw. Once you keep pushing, it gets easier. God helps us because He put the book of Numbers near the front. Once you finish that book, it gets easier. So finally I reached the end of the book of Revelations.

Did I understand everything? No.

But as I talk to God each day, and all through the day, He tells me things and answers many of my questions about what I am reading, hearing, or thinking.

Sometimes He tells me the address (book, chapter, and verse). For example, every time I looked at the clock it was 3:33. After a few days of this, I opened my Bible and looked in all the books of the Bible at chapter 3 and 33, verse 3.

When I got to Jeremiah 33:3 I felt in my heart this is what God was showing me:

> *"Call to Me, and I will answer you, and show you great and mighty things, which you do not know"* (NKJV).

Sometimes I hear the Lord tell me a Scripture reference, so I go to a Bible web-search program and sure enough, there is a Scripture saying the same thing.

I will not compromise my walk with the Lord. I know the importance and responsibility of being an ambassador for God.

I seek none of His glory or honor. I know I need to confirm what He is saying, but I know that I know His voice. I have heard it and followed it many times and proved it to be true.

Every day I learn more and more of His heart. I have learned that the Bible is a living Word and this means: When we have a relationship with the Author, we will receive deeper and deeper revelation.

Am I perfect? No way! However, He is.

As long as I hide in His glory, He covers me. Yes, almost immediately when I miss the mark, God will still stop me saying, "OK, time for your spiritual whipping."

He just hugs me and says, "You're learning, I love you."

I know we will only reach that place of perfection when we stand in front of Him. I have found that God is always teaching us. I attend Christian conferences and I watch webcasts from many of the speakers God has blessed us with today.

I have learned to take Jesus everywhere I go. If we are with someone, we get to know them better. Relationships grow until we begin seeing through their eyes.

I believe that since my God is the One who created every living thing, He really is the One who knows all the answers.

God loves you all! Be Blessed!

Scripture Index

Matthew 17:20   -- 39
Matthew 22:37   -- 63
Matthew 25:21   -- 104
Mark 16:15   -- 1652
Luke 7:21   -- 81
Luke 10:19   -- 55
John 1:14   -- 108
John 1:27   -- 40
John 14:12-14   -- 105
John 16:7   -- 92
John 17:22   -- 133
Acts 2:5-7, 11-12   -- 42
Acts 5:15-16   -- 121
Acts 16:31   -- 165
Acts 27:24   -- 91
Romans 8:32   -- 180
Romans 8:38-39   -- 180
Romans 14:11   -- 170
Romans 15:5-6   -- 93
1 Corinthians 2:9   -- 181
2 Corinthians 3:17   -- 107
2 Corinthians 3:18   -- 138
2 Corinthians 4:6   -- 137
2 Corinthians 4:6-7 -- 19
2 Corinthians 5:18   -- 84
2 Corinthians 10:3-4 -- 61
Ephesians 6:10-12   -- 47
Philippians 4:4-5   -- 40
Philippians 4:6-7   -- 41
Philippians 4:19   -- 23
Hebrews 11:6   -- 143
James 1:5-6   -- 115
1 Peter 3:15   -- 149
1 Peter 4:10-11   -- 104
1 Peter 5:6-7   -- 30
1 John 4:2-3   -- 77

Are You Ready for This?
by Joel and Cheryl Davis

"Oh my goodness, you are covered in gold dust!"

It sparkled in the light like glitter, but more brilliant. Some of the flecks were larger like glitter, and some of them were tiny like dust. It was on his skin, eyebrows, eyelashes, and shirt.

The day Dudley arrived at our door covered in gold dust set a new standard for the "normal Christian lifestyle."

We are blessed to have a Christian community equipped and empowered. A culture that takes Jesus everywhere we go—the grocery store, the workplace, and far beyond the walls of the church. We see more and more miracles as we grow in our Christian walk. It's an incredible adventure with the Lord, but we were about to get an upgrade.

As I write this on the 147 day of Dudley's gold manifestation, I am still in amazement at what God is doing. Even though it recurs daily, each day is always different and exciting. We have the privilege of being friends with Dudley and Natalie, as well as the privilege of sharing what God is doing with others as we steward the testimony of His goodness.

187

We talk to Dudley almost every day, and often several times a day to hear his latest testimony. We love his straightforward, no-nonsense approach, his fun-loving nature, and tender heart. He's the real deal. We share story after story; we laugh, cry, and marvel together as we give God the glory for his marvelous workings.

Natalie is so genuine, wise, and solid in her relationship with God. The entire Perio family is precious to us and a true joy to our hearts.

Dudley often tells people that God never gives all the pieces to one person, so that we must be in relationship with others. We are all part of God's family, working together, and bringing as many others alongside as we can. We honor everyone, and believe all are qualified. It is not gold dust that qualifies you, but rather it is the Holy Spirit living inside of you.

We have seen gold dust manifestations a few times before when we have been praying for people and sometimes during worship. This daily "gold dust" appearance on Dudley was a new turn. We knew it was pointing to each of us and how we live our daily walk with the Lord, and how He wants to reveal His glory through us. If we don't "shine," how else will the world know Him and His nature?

Arise, shine, for your light has come, and
the glory of the Lord rises upon you...
Nations will come to your light, and kings
to the brightness of your dawn.
                              —Isaiah 60:1, 3 NIV

Watching the hand of God move through Dudley's life has certainly changed a few things in our lives. We find ourselves falling more in love with people than ever, eagerly stepping out to demonstrate the love of God. As faith increases, what is possible also increases. Gigantic, God-sized dreams are opening up. We are bringing the Kingdom to every aspect of society and to the nations. As we dream with God for big things, we are equipping and empowering others to do the same. Life with Jesus is the most exciting life ever. Why should we settle for anything less than all of Him? In Him there is fullness of joy!

You will make known to me the path of
life; In Your presence is fullness of joy;
In Your right hand there are pleasures
forever.
                              —Psalm 16:11 NASB

Miracles teach us how to see. We learn how to see God, how to see others, and how to partner with the Lord in what He has called us to do.

In the book of Revelations, it says that the testimony of Jesus is the spirit of prophecy. In reading this testimony of what Jesus is doing, you have received a prophetic opportunity: If He did it once, He will do it again.

As Dudley steps out to pray for people, he is seeing God move in their lives, and so are we. To those who will receive it, you have been handed a baton.

I encourage you to run the joyous race and dive into the adventure of living the "normal Christian lifestyle."

Your hunger for more will take you places in the living God that reveal the beautiful glory of our Jesus, and reveal the amazing and wonderful people around you!

There is absolutely nothing like Him and this life He has called us to!

> *For the anxious longing of the creation waits eagerly for the revealing of the sons of God.*
> —Romans 8:19 NASB

Let the adventure begin.

Acknowledgments
from Dudley Perio

I want to thank Jesus for His mercy and grace and sending an army of angels to save me. Great and mighty is the Lord God Almighty. He is the love of my heart and I will praise Him all my days.

I want to thank my wife, Natalie, and my children: Daniel, Sarah, Nathan, Kenny, Natalie Ann, Clara, and my daughter-in-law, Mary, for their encouragement, love, and prayers. My desire is to always see them chasing God.

I want to thank Paul and Lynn Crawford for hearing God and stepping out to make this book possible. Their dedication in spending their lives, money, and prayers to help others get the message of God's love truly reflects in all they do. Their efforts have captured my heart throughout this book.

I want to thank Cheryl and Joel Davis for their help in recording the hours and hours of these testimonies. I thank them for the prayers and opening up their lives and home to document God's love for his people.

I want to thank Pastor Bill Hart for being real and letting the love of Jesus shine. He carries such a heart for God. Freedom rings in his church, Cathedral of Praise. I thank him for all the time he has spent in the DVD's and CD's. His heart beats one with Jesus.

I want to thank Seth Carson and all my friends for all their hidden work in helping get the book, DVD's, and CD's done.

I want to thank Paul, Lynn, Cheryl, Joel, and Bill for all the love and encouragement they have poured throughout these exciting days. I now know why they are God-chasers and nation-changers.

I pray that each one receives the supernatural blessing from God. I thank you all from my heart, soul, and spirit.

Acknowledgments
from Paul & Lynn Crawford

Our greatest thank you is to God, The Author of Salvation. His empowering and step-by-step leading of the Holy Spirit made this book possible. We discovered an ease in the writing process as we sat in His presence and listened to His voice. I can hardly wait for the next book He has for us. We want to thank all of you who trudged through the tedious editing process. Rejoice! It is well worth it.

We want to thank our Austin Family in faith. They opened their hearts and homes to us. They gave us a much needed hand and introduced us to real Tex-Mex. Fantastic! God surprised us. He gave us a love for each other before we even met face-to-face. We love you all.

Much thanks to our dear friend and courageous editor, Elaine Wright Colvin, for never blocking our calls, and for joining us in another "instant book." And most importantly, for her great love for God and His Word. We love you, Elaine. We are becoming better writers for Jesus because of you.

We thank Dudley for listening and acting on God's leading. He and Natalie overflow with God's love for others.

God led us to write this book and enabled us beyond our natural abilities. We give all the glory to God.

> *The Lord gave the word: Great was the company of those who proclaimed it.*
> —Psalm 68:11 NKJV

Dudley Perio

"Just an ordinary guy"

Dudley Perio is well known in the Texas oil fields for his designs and inventions, as well as for thirty years as an oil rig engineer. He is the founder Dudley J. Perio, Inc. of Austin, which designs, manufactures, and markets oil field equipment for the oil and gas industry.

Since September 5, 2010, God has been taking Dudley on an amazing journey to do "His" bidding to let people know that God loves them. As well as healings, miracles, words of knowledge, preaching, and encouraging, God has now imparted to Dudley "gold dust." This daily recurrence is all about praising God and being in his Manifest Presence. With the "gold dust" comes questions by onlookers, God's speaking to Dudley about a person's need, and a supernatural gift of faith that allows the ministry of healing to take place.

To learn more about God's working through Dudley Perio and what is happening in and around Austin, Texas, or to contact Dudley, follow him on: "What Is God Doing In Austin" Website & Blog which has been set up to:

(1) record and inform you about expected revival in Austin, Texas;

(2) share the ongoing story of Dudley Perio and provide a weekly blog of how God is working through Dudley.

http://whatisgoddoinginaustin.info/index.php

To contact Dudley or invitations, e*mail:*

info@whatisgoddoinginaustin.info

Paul and Lynn Crawford

"Ordinary Christians
Doing Extraordinary Works"

Paul and Lynn Crawford have been in full-time ministry for over thirty years. Paul's calling is "to spread the Gospel through video to teach, train, evangelize, and bring healing." Through the ministry International Television & Evangelism Center (ITEC), they've produced over a million DVDs, CDs, and live webcast conferences on the Internet at: www.OneInTheSpirit.tv

Lynn has been active in her church, Women's Aglow leadership, and has served on an Aglow regional board. After years of serving Charles and Francis Hunter, they developed "God's Healing Power Through You" seminars. The Crawford's have taught this seminar in many nations on over 100 international trips

Their previously published books include: God's *Healing Power Through You*; and *Embracing Grace Now!; Living In God's Glory* is their latest book.

Paul and Lynn live in Kingston, Washington, a ferry ride west of Seattle. They have six

children, ten grandchildren, and attend
Bayside Community Church.

Contact for Recorded Media,
Books or Speaking invitations

Paul and Lynn Crawford

godshealingpower@gmail.com

www.OneInTheSpirit.tv

To our reader,

Did God speak to you through the reading of
this book? Have you glimpsed the possibilities
of "Living in God's Glory" and experiencing an
adventure with God as you hear and respond to
His Voice?

Are you aware of divine encounters, miracles,
healings in your life, your city, or beyond as a
result of taking the Gospel to the Nations?

We'd love to hear from you. We want to praise
God with you as you give testimony to what He
is doing in your life.
Please email us at:
    godshealingpower@gmail.com
Or send a snail mail letter to:
    New Sound Media
    PO Box 7300
    Kingston, WA 98346

Contact or Recorded Media

For Crawford's Books or Speaking

Paul and Lynn Crawford

New Sound Media
PO Box 7300
Kingston, WA 98346
Email: godshealingpower@gmail.com
www.OneInTheSpirit.tv

For Dudley Perio CDs and DVDs
www.whatisgoddoinginaustin.info

To Contact Dudley
info@whatisgoddoinginaustin.info

Prophet Kobus/SpiritWord,
16,000 cripples healed in last 9 years

Books, CDs & DVDs for North America
Available online at:
http://oneinthespirit.tv/spiritword

New media listings are posted on the
website each month